Mankind and Political Arithmetic

by Sir William Petty

Contents:

INTRODUCTION.

William Petty, born on the 26th of May, 1623, was the son of a clothier at Romsey in Hampshire. After education at the Romsey Grammar School, he continued his studies at Caen in Normandy. There he supported himself by a little trade while learning French, and advancing his knowledge of Greek, Latin, Mathematics, and much else that belonged to his idea of a liberal education. His idea was large. He came back to England, and had for a short time a place in the Navy; but at the age of twenty he went abroad again, and was away three years, studying actively at Utrecht, Leyden, and Amsterdam, and also in Paris. In Paris he assisted Thomas Hobbes in drawing diagrams for his treatise on optics. At the age of twenty- four Petty took out a patent for the invention of a copying machine. It was described in a folio pamphlet "On Double Writing." That was in 1647, in Civil War time, and although Petty followed Hobbes in his studies, he did not share the philosopher's political opinions, but held with the Parliament. In 1648 he added to his former pamphlet a "Declaration concerning the newly invented Art of Double Writing."

Samuel Hartlib, the large-hearted Pole, who in those days spent his worldly means in England for the advancement of agriculture and of education, and other aids to the well-being of a nation, had caused Milton to write his letter on education, as has been shown in the Introduction to the hundred and twenty-first volume of this Library, which contains that Letter together with Milton's

Areopagitica. Young Petty's first published writing was a Letter to Hartlib on Education, entitled "The Advice of W. P. to Mr. Samuel Hartlib for the Advancement of some Particular Parts of Learning." This appeared in 1648, when Petty's age was twenty-five, and its aim was to suggest a wider view of the whole field of education than had been possible in the Middle Ages, of which schools and colleges were then preserving the traditions, as they do still here and there to some extent. This pamphlet has been reprinted in the sixth volume of the "Harleian Miscellany." William Petty wished the training of the young to be in several respects more practical.

His own activity of mind caused him to settle at Oxford, where he taught anatomy and chemistry, which he had been studying abroad. He had read with Hobbes the writings of Vesalius, the great founder of modern practical anatomy. In 1649 William Petty graduated at Oxford as Doctor of Medicine, obtained a fellowship at Brasenose, and practised. In 1650 he surprised the public by restoring the action of the lungs in a woman who had been hanged for infanticide, and so restoring her to life.

Dr. Petty now took his place at Oxford among the energetic men of science who had been inspired by the teaching of Francis Bacon to seek knowledge by direct experiment, and to value knowledge above all things for its power of advancing the welfare of man. The headquarters of these workers were at Oxford, and in London at Gresham College.

In 1650 Petty was made Professor of Anatomy at Oxford, and it is a characteristic illustration of his great activity of mind that he was at the same time Professor of Music at Gresham College. Music had then a high place in the Seven Sciences, as that use of regulated numbers which expressed the harmonies of the created world. The Seven Sciences were divided into three of the Trivium, and four of the Quadrivium. The three of the Trivium concerned the use of speech; they were Grammar, Rhetoric, and Logic. The four of the Quadrivium concerned number and measure; they were Arithmetic, Geometry, Music; and Astronomy, which led up straight to God. Advance to Music might be represented in the student's mind by his teaching to a sense of the harmonious relation of all his studies, which, so to speak, lived in his mind as a single well-proportioned thought.

In 1652 Dr. Petty was sent to Ireland as physician to the army of the Commonwealth. While there his active mind observed that the Survey on which the Government had based its distribution of fortified lands to the soldiers had been "most inefficiently and absurdly managed." He obtained the commission to make a fresh Survey, which he completed accurately in thirteen months, and by which he obtained in payments from the Government and from other persons interested ten thousand pounds. By investing this in the purchase of soldiers' claims, he secured for himself an Irish estate of fifty thousand acres in the county of Kerry, opened upon it mines and quarries, developed trade in timber, and set up a fishery. John Evelyn said of him "that he had never known such another genius, and that if Evelyn were a prince he would make Petty his second councillor at least." Henry Cromwell as Lord Deputy in Ireland made Petty his secretary.

Petty's Maps were printed in 1685, two years before his death, as "Hiberniae Delineatio quoad hactenus licuit perfectissima;" a collection of thirty-six maps, with a portrait of Sir William Petty, a work answering to its description as the most perfect delineation of Ireland that had up to that time been obtained. There is a coloured copy of Petty's maps in the British Museum, and also an uncoloured copy, with the first five maps varying from those in the coloured copy, and giving a General Map of Ireland, followed by Maps of Leinster, Munster, Ulster, and Connaught. There was afterwards published in duodecimo, without date, "A Geographical Description of ye Kingdom of Ireland, collected from ye actual Survey made by Sir William Petty, corrected and amended, engraven and published by Fra. Lamb." This volume gives as its contents, "one general mapp, four provincial mapps, and thirty-two county mapps; to which is added a mapp of Great Brittaine and Ireland, together with an Index of the whole."

At the Restoration William Petty accepted the inevitable change, and continued his service to the country. He was knighted by Charles the Second, and appointed in 1661 Inspector-General of Ireland. He entered Parliament. He was one of the first founders of the Royal Society, established at the beginning of the reign of Charles the Second; and the outcome of these scientific studies along the line marked out by Francis Bacon, which had been actively pursued in Oxford and at Gresham College. In 1663 he applied his ingenuity to the invention of a swift double-bottomed ship, that made one or two passages between England and Ireland, but was then lost in a storm.

In 1670 Sir William Petty established on his lands at Kerry the English settlement at the head of the bay of Kenmare. The building of forty-two houses for the English settlers first laid the foundations of the present town of Kenmare. "The population," writes Lord Macaulay, "amounted to a hundred and eighty. The land round the town was well cultivated. The cattle were numerous. Two small barks were employed in fishing and trading along the coast. The supply of herrings, pilchards, mackerel, and salmon, was plentiful, and would have been still more plentiful had not the beach been, in the finest part of the year, covered by multitudes of seals, which preyed on the fish of the bay. Yet the seal was not an unwelcome visitor: his fur was valuable; and his oil supplied light through the long nights of winter. An attempt was made with great success to set up ironworks. It was not yet the practice to employ coal for the purpose of smelting; and the manufacturers of Kent and Sussex had much difficulty in procuring timber at a reasonable price. The neighbourhood of Kenmare was then richly wooded; and Petty found it a gainful speculation to send ore thither." He looked also for profit from the variegated marbles of adjacent islands. Distant two days' journey over the mountains from the nearest English, Petty's English settlement of Kenmare withstood all surrounding dangers, and in 1688, a year after its founder's death, defended itself successfully against a fierce and general attack.

Sir William Petty died at London, on the 16th of December, 1687, and was buried in his native town of Romsey. He had added to his great wealth by marriage, and was the founder of the family in which another Sir William Petty became Earl of Shelburne and first Marquis of Lansdowne. The son of that first Marquis was Henry third Marquis of Lansdowne, who took a conspicuous part in our political history during the present century.

Sir William Petty's survey of the land in Ireland, called the Down Survey, because its details were set down in maps, remains the legal record of the title on which half the land in Ireland is held. The original maps are preserved in the Public Record Office at Dublin, and many of Petty's MSS. are in the Bodleian Library at Oxford.

He published in 1662 and 1685 a "Treatise of Taxes and Contributions, the same being frequently to the present state and affairs of Ireland," of which his view started from the general opinion that men should contribute to the public charge according to their interest in the public peace--that is, according to their riches. "Now, he said, "there are two sorts of riches--one actual, and the other potential. A man is actually and truly rich according to what he eateth, drinketh, weareth, or in any other way really and actually enjoyeth. Others are but potentially and imaginatively rich, who though they have power over much, make little use of it, these being rather stewards and exchangers for the other sort than owners for themselves." He then showed how he considered that "every man ought to contribute according to what he taketh to himself, and actually enjoyeth."

In 1674 Sir William Petty published a paper on "Duplicate Proportion," and in 1679 he published in Latin a "Colloquy of David with his Own Soul." In 1682 he published a tract called "Quantulumcunque, concerning Money;" and "England's Guide to Industry," in 1686. From 1682 to 1687, the year of his death, Sir William Petty was drawing great attention to the "Essays on Political Arithmetic," which are here reprinted. There was the little "Essay in Political Arithmetic, concerning the People, Housings, Hospitals of London and Paris;" published in 1682, again in French in 1686, and again in English in 1687. There was the little "Essay concerning the Multiplication of Mankind, together with an Essay on the Growth of London," published in 1682, and again in 1683 and 1686. There was in 1683, "Another Essay in Political Arithmetic concerning the growth of the City of London." There were "Farther Considerations on the Dublin Bills of Mortality," in 1686; and "Five Essays on

Political Arithmetic" (in French and English), "Observations upon the Cities of London and Rome," in 1687, the last year of Sir William Petty's life. Other writings of his were published in his lifetime, or have been published since his death. He was in the study of political economy one of the most ingenious and practical thinkers before the days of Adam Smith.

But the interest of those "Essays in Political Arithmetic" lies chiefly in the facts presented by so trustworthy an authority. London had become in the time of the Stuarts the most populous city in Europe, if not in the world. This Sir William Petty sought to prove against the doubts of foreign and other critics, and his "Political Arithmetic" was an endeavour to determine the relative strength in population of the chief cities of England, France, and Holland. His application of arithmetic in the first of these essays to a census of the population at the Day of Judgment he himself spoke of slightingly. It is a curious example of a bygone form of theological discussion. But his tables and his reasonings upon them grow in interest as he attempts his numbering of the people in the reign of James II. by collecting facts upon which his deductions might be founded. The references to the deaths by Plague in London before the cleansing of the town by the great fire of 1666 are very suggestive; and in one passage there is incidental note of delay in the coming of the Plague then due, without reckoning the change made in conditions of health by the rebuilding. Nobody knew, and no one even now can calculate, how many lives the Fire of London saved.

There was in Petty's time no direct numbering of the people. The first census in this country was not until more than a hundred years after Sir William Petty's death, although he points out in these essays how easily it could be established, and what useful information it would give. There was a census taken at Rome 566 years before Christ. But the first census in Great Britain was taken in 1801, under provision of an Act passed on the last day of the year 1800, to secure a numbering of the population every ten years. Ireland was not included in the return; the first census in Ireland was not until the year 1813.

Sir William Petty had to base his calculations partly upon the Bills of

Mortality, which had been imperfectly begun under Elizabeth, but fell into disuse, and were revived, as a weekly record of the number of deaths, beginning on the 29th of October, 1603; notices of diseases first appeared in them in 1629. The weekly bills were published every Thursday, and any householder could have them supplied to him for four shillings a year. These essays will show how inferences as to the number of the living were drawn from the number of the dead. And even now our Political Arithmetic depends too much upon rough calculations made from the death register. It is seven years since the last census; we have lost count of the changes in our population to a very great extent, and have to wait three years before our reckoning can be made sure. The interval should be reduced to five years.

Another of Sir William Petty's helps in the arithmetic of population was the Chimney Tax, a revival of the old fumage or hearth-money-- smoke farthings, as the people called them--once paid, according to Domesday Book, for every chimney in a house. Charles the Second had set up a chimney tax in the year 1662; the statistics of the collection were at the service of Sir William Petty. The tax outlived him but two years. It was promptly abolished in the first year of William and Mary.

The interest taken at home and abroad in these calculations of Political Arithmetic set other men calculating, and reasoning upon their calculations. The next worker in that direction was Gregory King, Lancaster Herald, whose calculations immediately followed those of Sir William Petty. Sir William Petty's essays extended from 1682 until his death in 1687. Gregory King's estimates were made in 1689. They were a study of the number population and distribution of wealth among us at the time of the English Revolution, and the unpublished results were first printed in a chapter on "The People of England," which formed part a volume published in 1699 as "An Essay upon the Probable Methods of making a People Gainers in the Balance of Trade, by the Author of the Essay on Ways and Means." The volume was written by a member of Parliament in the days of William and Mary, who desired to apply principles of political economy to the maintenance of English wealth and liberty. It has been wrongly scribed to Defoe; and its suggestion of the plan a trading Corporation for solution of the whole problem of relief to the poor who cannot work, and relief from the poor who can, might indeed make another chapter in Defoe's "Essay on Projects." The chapter, which gives the Political Arithmetic of Gregory King, with such comment and suggestions as might be expected from a liberal supporter of the Revolution, and with this suggestion of a Corporation, is in itself a complete essay. It follows naturally upon the Political Arithmetic of Sir William Petty in close sequence of time, and in carrying a like method of inquiry forward until it reaches a few more conclusions. I have, therefore, added it to this volume. It seems, at any rate, to show how Sir William Petty's books, of which the very small size grieved the stationer, had a large influence on other minds; his figures bearing fruit in a new search for facts and careful reasoning on the condition of the country at one of the most critical times in English history.

H. M.

THE STATIONER TO THE READER

The ensuing essay concerning the growth of the city of London was entitled "Another Essay," intimating that some other essay had preceded it, which was not to be found. I having been much importuned for that precedent essay, have found that the same was about the growth, increase, and multiplication of mankind, which subject should in order of nature precede that of the growth of the city of London, but am not able to procure the essay itself, only I have obtained from a gentleman, who sometimes corresponded with Sir W. Petty, an extract of a letter from Sir William to him, which I verily believe containeth the scope thereof; wherefore, I must desire the reader to be content therewith, till more can be had.

The extract of a letter concerning the scope of an essay intended to precede another essay concerning the growth of the City of London, &c. An Essay in Political Arithmetic, concerning the value and increase of People and Colonies.

The scope of this essay is concerning people and colonies, and to make way for "Another Essay" concerning the growth of the city of London. I desire in this first essay to give the world some light concerning the numbers of people in England, with Wales, and in Ireland; as also of the number of houses and families wherein they live, and of acres they occupy.

2. How many live upon their lands, how many upon their personal estates and commerce, and how many upon art, and labour; how many upon alms, how many upon offices and public employments, and how many as cheats and thieves; how many are impotents, children, and decrepit old men.

3. How many upon the poll-taxes in England, do pay extraordinary rates, and how many at the level.

4. How many men and women are prolific, and how many of each are married or unmarried.

5. What the value of people are in England, and what in Ireland at a medium, both as members of the Church or Commonwealth, or as slaves and servants to one another; with a method how to estimate the same, in any other country or colony.

6. How to compute the value of land in colonies, in comparison to England and Ireland.

7. How 10,000 people in a colony may be planted to the best advantage.

8. A conjecture in what number of years England and Ireland may be fully peopled, as also all America, and lastly the whole habitable earth.

9. What spot of the earth's globe were fittest for a general and universal emporium, whereby all the people thereof may best enjoy one another's labours and commodities.

10. Whether the speedy peopling of the earth would make

(1) For the good of mankind.

(2) To fulfil the revealed will of God.

(3) To what prince or State the same would be most advantageous.

11. An exhortation to all thinking men to solve the Scriptures and other good histories, concerning the number of people in all ages of the world, in the great cities thereof, and elsewhere.

12. An appendix concerning the different number of sea-fish and wild-fowl at the end of every thousand years since Noah's Flood.

13. An hypothesis of the use of those spaces (of about 8,000 miles through) within the globe of our earth, supposing a shell of 150 miles thick.

14. What may be the meaning of glorified bodies, in case the place of the blessed shall be without the convex of the orb of the fixed stars, if that the whole system of the world was made for the use of our earth's men.

THE PRINCIPAL POINTS OF THIS DISCOURSE

1. That London doubles in forty years, and all England in three hundred and sixty years.

2. That there be, A.D. 1682, about 670,000 souls in London, and about 7,400,000 in all England and Wales, and about 28,000,000 of acres of profitable land.

3. That the periods of doubling the people are found to be, in all degrees, from between ten to twelve hundred years.

4. That the growth of London must stop of itself before the year 1800.

5. A table helping to understand the Scriptures, concerning the number of people mentioned in them.

6. That the world will be fully peopled within the next two thousand years.

7. Twelve ways whereby to try any proposal pretended for the public good.

8. How the city of London may be made (morally speaking) invincible.

9. A help to uniformity in religion.

10. That it is possible to increase mankind by generation four times more than at present.

11. The plagues of London is the chief impediment and objection against the

growth of the city.

12. That an exact account of the people is necessary in this matter.

OF THE GROWTH OF THE CITY OF LONDON: And of the Measures, Periods, Causes, and Consequences thereof

By the city of London we mean the housing within the walls of the old city, with the liberties thereof, Westminster, the Borough of Southwark, and so much of the built ground in Middlesex and Surrey, whose houses are contiguous unto, or within call of those aforementioned. Or else we mean the housing which stand upon the ninety-seven parishes within the walls of London; upon the sixteen parishes next without them; the six parishes of Westminster, and the fourteen out-parishes in Middlesex and Surrey, contiguous to the former, all which, 133 parishes, are comprehended within the weekly bills of mortality.

The growth of this city is measured. (1) By the quantity of ground, or number of acres upon which it stands. (2) By the number of houses, as the same appears by the hearth-books and late maps. (3) By the cubical content of the said housing. (4) By the flooring of the same. (5) By the number of days' work, or charge of building the said houses. (6) By the value of the said houses, according to their yearly rent, and number of years' purchase. (7) By the number of inhabitants; according to which latter sense only we make our computations in this essay.

Till a better rule can be obtained, we conceive that the proportion of the people may be sufficiently measured by the proportion of the burials in such years as were neither remarkable for extraordinary healthfulness or sickliness.

That the city hath increased in this latter sense appears from the bills of mortality represented in the two following tables, viz., one whereof is a continuation for eighteen years, ending 1682, of that table which was published in the 117th page of the book of the observations upon the London bills of mortality, printed in the year 1676. The other showeth what number of people died at a medium of two years, indifferently taken, at about twenty years' distance from each other.

The first of the said two tables.

A.D. 97 16 Out Buried Besides of Christened Parishes Parishes Parishes in all the Plague 1665 5,320 12,463 10,925 28,708 68,596 9,967 1666 1,689 3,969 5,082 10,740 1,998 8,997 1667 761 6,405 8,641 15,807 35 10,938 1668 796 6,865 9,603 17,267 14 11,633 1669 1,323 7,500 10,440 19,263 3 12,335 1670 1,890 7,808 10,500 20,198 11,997 1671 1,723 5,938 8,063 15,724 5 12,510 1672 2,237 6,788 9,200 18,225 5 12,593 1673 2,307 6,302 8,890 17,499 5 11,895 1674 2,801 7,522 10,875 21,198 3 11,851 1675 2,555 5,986 8,702 17,243 1 11,775 1676 2,756 6,508 9,466 18,730 2 12,399 1677 2,817 6,632 9,616 19,065 2 12,626 1678 3,060 6,705 10,908 20,673 5 12,601 1679 3,074 7,481 11,173 21,728 2 12,288 1680 3,076 7,066 10,911 21,053 12,747 1681 3,669 8,136 12,166 23,971 13,355 1682 2,975 7,009 10,707 20,691 12,653

According to which latter table there died as follows:-

THE LATTER OF THE SAID TWO TABLES

There died in London at the medium between the years -

1604 and 1605 . . . 5,135. A. 1621 and 1622 . . . 8,527. B. 1641 and 1642 . . . 11,883. C. 1661 and 1662 . . . 15,148. D. 1681 and 1682 . . . 22,331. E.

Wherein observe, that the number C is double to A and 806 over. That D is double to B within 1,906. That C and D is double to A and B within 293. That E is double to C within 1,435. That D and E is double to B and C within 3,341; and that C and D and E are double to A and B and C within 1,736; and that E is above quadruple to A. All which differences (every way considered) do allow the doubling of the people of London in 40 years to be a sufficient estimate thereof in round numbers, and without the trouble of fractions. We also say that 669,930 is near the number of people now in London, because the burials are 22,331, which, multiplied by 30 (one dying yearly out of 30, as appears in the 94th page of the aforementioned observations), maketh the said number; and because there are 84,000 tenanted houses (as we are credibly informed), which, at 8 in each, makes 672,000 souls; the said two accounts differing inconsiderably from each other.

We have thus pretty well found out in what number of years (viz., in about 40) that the city of London hath doubled, and the present number of inhabitants to be about 670,000. We must now also endeavour the same for the whole territory of England and Wales. In order whereunto, we first say that the assessment of London is about an eleventh part of the whole territory, and, therefore, that the people of the whole may well be eleven times that of London, viz., about 7,369,000 souls; with which account that of the poll-money, hearth-money, and the bishop's late numbering of the communicants, do pretty well agree; wherefore, although the said number of 7,369,000 be not (as it cannot be) a demonstrated truth, yet it will serve for a good supposition, which is as much as we want at present.

As for the time in which the people double, it is yet more hard to be found. For we have good experience (in the said page 94 of the aforementioned observations) that in the country but 1 of 50 die per annum; and by other late accounts, that there have been sometimes but 24 births for 23 burials. The which two points, if they were universally and constantly true, there would be colour enough to say that the people doubled but in about 1,200 years. As, for example, suppose there be 600 people, of which let a fiftieth part die per annum, then there shall die 12 per annum; and if the births be as 24 to 23, then the increase of the people shall be somewhat above half a man per annum, and consequently the supposed number of 600 cannot be doubled but in 1,126 years, which, to reckon in round numbers, and for that the aforementioned fractions were not exact, we had rather call 1,200.

There are also other good observations, that even in the country one in about

30 or 32 per annum hath died, and that there have been five births for four burials. Now, according to this doctrine, 20 will die per annum out of the above 600, and 25 will be born, so as the increase will be five, which is a hundred and twentieth part of the said 600. So as we have two fair computations, differing from each other as one to ten; and there are also several other good observations for other measures.

I might here insert, that although the births in this last computation be 25 of 600, or a twenty-fourth part of the people, yet that in natural possibility they may be near thrice as many, and near 75. For that by some late observations, the teeming females between 15 and 44 are about 180 of the said 600, and the males of between 18 and 59 are about 180 also, and that every teeming woman can bear a child once in two years; from all which it is plain that the births may be 90 (and abating 15 for sickness, young abortions, and natural barrenness), there may remain 75 births, which is an eighth of the people, which by some observations we have found to be but a two-and-thirtieth part, or but a quarter of what is thus shown to be naturally possible. Now, according to this reckoning, if the births may be 75 of 600, and the burials but 15, then the annual increase of the people will be 60; and so the said 600 people may double in ten years, which differs yet more from 1,200 above- mentioned. Now, to get out of this difficulty, and to temper those vast disagreements, I took the medium of 50 and 30 dying per annum, and pitched upon 40; and I also took the medium between 24 births and 23 burials, and 5 births for 4 burials, viz., allowing about 10 births for 9 burials; upon which supposition there must die 15 per annum out of the above-mentioned 600, and the births must be 16 and two-thirds, and the increase one and two-thirds, or five-thirds of a man, which number, compared with 1,800 thirds, or 600 men, gives 360 years for the time of doubling (including some allowance for wars, plagues, and famines, the effects thereof), though they be terrible at the times and places where they happen, yet in a period of 360 years is no great matter in the whole nation. For the plagues of England in twenty years have carried away scarce an eightieth part of the people of the whole nation; and the late ten years' civil wars (the like whereof hath not been in several ages before) did not take away above a fortieth part of the whole people.

According to which account or measure of doubling, if there be now in England and Wales 7,400,000 people, there were about 5,526,000 in the beginning of Queen Elizabeth's reign, A.D. 1560, and about 2,000,000 at the Norman Conquest, of which consult the Doomsday Book, and my Lord Hale's "Origination of Mankind."

Memorandum.--That if the people double in 360 years, that the present 320,000,000 computed by some learned men (from the measures of all the nations of the world, their degrees of being peopled, and good accounts of the people in several of them) to be now upon the face of the earth, will within the next 2,000 years so increase as to give one head for every two acres of land in the habitable part of the earth. And then, according to the prediction of the Scriptures, there must be wars, and great slaughter, &c.

Wherefore, as an expedient against the above-mentioned difference between 10 and 1,200 years, we do for the present, and in this country, admit of 360 years to be the time wherein the people of England do double, according to the present laws and practice of marriages.

Now, if the city double its people in 40 years, and the present number be 670,000, and if the whole territory be 7,400,000, and double in 360 years, as aforesaid, then by the underwritten table it appears that A.D. 1840 the people of the city will be 10,718,880, and those of the whole country but 10,917,389, which is but inconsiderably more. Wherefore it is certain and necessary that the growth of the city must stop before the said year 1840, and will be at its utmost height in the next preceding period, A.D. 1800, when the number of the city will be eight times its present number, 5,359,000. And when (besides the said number) there will be 4,466,000 to perform the tillage, pasturage, and other rural works necessary to be done without the said city, as by the following table, viz.:-

A.D. Burials People in People in London England 1565 2,568 77,040 5,526,929 As in the } 1605 5,135 former table } 1642 11,883 } 1682 22,331

669,930 7,369,230 1722 44,662 1762 89,324 1802 178,648 5,359,440
9,825,650 1842 357,296 10,718,889 10,917,389

Now, when the people of London shall come to be so near the people of all
England, then it follows that the growth of London must stop before the said
year 1842, as aforesaid, and must be at its greatest height A.D. 1800, when it
will be eight times more than now, with above 4,000,000 for the service of the
country and ports, as aforesaid.

Of the aforementioned vast difference between 10 years and 1,200 years for
doubling the people, we make this use, viz.:- To justify the Scriptures and all
other good histories concerning the number of the people in ancient time. For
supposing the eight persons who came out of the Ark, increased by a
progressive doubling in every ten years, might grow in the first 100 years after
the Flood from 8 to 8,000, and that in 350 years after the Flood (whereabouts
Noah died) to 1,000,000 and by this time, 1682, to 320,000,000 (which by
rational conjecture are thought to be now in the world), it will not be hard to
compute how, in the intermediate years, the growths may be made, according
to what is set down in the following table, wherein making the doubling to be
ten years at first, and within 1,200 years at last, we take a discretionary liberty,
but justifiable by observations and the Scriptures for the rest, which table we
leave to be corrected by historians who know the bigness of ancient cities,
armies, and colonies in the respective ages of the world, in the meantime
affirming that without such difference in the measures and periods for
doubling (the extremes whereof we have demonstrated to be real and true) it is
impossible to solve what is written in the Holy Scriptures and other authentic
books. For if we pitch upon any one number throughout for this purpose, 150
years is the fittest of all round numbers; according to which there would have
been but 512 souls in the whole world in Moses' time (being 800 years after
the Flood), when 603,000 Israelites of above twenty years old (besides those
of other ages, tribes, and nations) were found upon an exact survey appointed
by God, whereas our table makes 12,000,000. And there would have been
about 8,000 in David's time, when were found 1,100,000, of above twenty
years old (besides others, as aforesaid) in Israel, upon the survey instigated by

Satan, whereas our table makes 32,000,000. And there would have been but a quarter of a million about the birth of Christ, or Augustus's time, when Rome and the Roman Empire were so great, whereas our table makes 100,000,000. Where note, that the Israelites in about 500 years, between their coming out of Egypt to David's reign, increased from 603,000 to 1,100,000.

On the other hand, if we pitch upon a less number, as 100 years, the world would have been over-peopled 700 years since. Wherefore no one number will solve the phenomena, and therefore we have supposed several, in order to make the following table, which we again desire historians to correct, according to what they find in antiquity concerning the number of the people in each age and country of the world.

We did (not long since) assist a worthy divine, writing against some sceptics, who would have baffled our belief of the resurrection, by saying, that the whole globe of the earth could not furnish matter enough for all the bodies that must rise at the last day, much less would the surface of the earth furnish footing for so vast a number; whereas we did (by the method afore mentioned) assert the number of men now living, and also of those that had died since the beginning of the world, and did withal show, that half the island of Ireland would afford them all, not only footing to stand upon, but graves to lie down in, for that whole number; and that two mountains in that country were as weighty as all the bodies that had ever been from the beginning of the world to the year 1680, when this dispute happened. For which purpose I have digressed from my intended purpose to insert this matter, intending to prosecute this hint further upon some more proper occasion.

A TABLE SHOWING HOW THE PEOPLE MIGHT HAVE DOUBLED IN THE SEVERAL AGES OF THE WORLD.

A.D., after the Flood. Periods of { 1 8 persons. doubling { 10 16 { 20 32 { 30 64 { 40 128 In 10 years { 50 256 { 60 512 { 70 1,024 { 80 2,048 { 90 4,096 { 100 8,000 and more. { 120 years after In 20 years { the Flood. 16,000 { 140 32,000 { 170 64,000 30 { { 200 128,000 40 240 256,000 50 290 512,000 60

350 1,000,000 and more. 70 420 2,000,000 100 520 4,000,000 190 710 8,000,000 290 1,000 16,000,000 in Moses' time. 400 1,400 32,000,000 about David's time. 550 1,950 64,000,000 750 2,700 128,000,000 about the birth of Christ. 1,000 3,700 256,000,000 300 { In { 4,000 320,000,000 1,200 {

It is here to be noted, that in this table we have assigned a different number of years for the time of doubling the people in the several ages of the world, and might have done the same for the several countries of the world, and therefore the said several periods assigned to the whole world in the lump may well enough consist with the 360 years especially assigned to England, between this day and the Norman Conquest; and the said 360 years may well enough serve for a supposition between this time and that of the world's being fully peopled; nor do we lay any stress upon one or the other in this disquisition concerning the growth of the city of London.

We have spoken of the growth of London, with the measures and periods thereof; we come next to the causes and consequences of the same.

The causes of its growth from 1642 to 1682 may be said to have been as follows, viz.:- From 1642 to 1650, that men came out of the country to London, to shelter themselves from the outrages of the Civil Wars during that time; from 1650 to 1660, the royal party came to London for their more private and inexpensive living; from 1660 to 1670, the king's friends and party came to receive his favours after his happy restoration; from 1670 to 1680, the frequency of plots and parliaments might bring extraordinary numbers to the city; but what reasons to assign for the like increase from 1604 to 1642 I know not, unless I should pick out some remarkable accident happening in each part of the said period, and make that to be the cause of this increase (as vulgar people make the cause of every man's sickness to be what he did last eat), wherefore, rather than so to say quidlibet de quolibet, I had rather quit even what I have above said to be the cause of London's increase from 1642 to 1682, and put the whole upon some natural and spontaneous benefits and advantages that men find by living in great more than in small societies, and shall therefore seek for the antecedent causes of this growth in the consequences of the like, considered in greater characters and proportions.

Now, whereas in arithmetic, out of two false positions the truth is extracted, so I hope out of two extravagant contrary suppositions to draw forth some solid and consistent conclusion, viz.:-

The first of the said two suppositions is, that the city of London is seven times bigger than now, and that the inhabitants of it are 4,690,000 people, and that in all the other cities, ports, towns, and villages, there are but 2,710,000 more.

The other supposition is, that the city of London is but a seventh part of its present bigness, and that the inhabitants of it are but 96,000, and that the rest of the inhabitants (being 7,304,000) do cohabit thus: 104,000 of them in small cities and towns, and that the rest, being 7,200,000, do inhabit in houses not contiguous to one another, viz., in 1,200,000 houses, having about twenty-four acres of ground belonging to each of them, accounting about 28,000,000 of acres to be in the whole territory of England, Wales, and the adjacent islands, which any man that pleases may examine upon a good map.

Now, the question is, in which of these two imaginary states would be the most convenient, commodious, and comfortable livings?

But this general question divides itself into the several questions, relating to the following particulars, viz.:-

1. For the defence of the kingdom against foreign powers.

2. For preventing the intestine commotions of parties and factions.

3. For peace and uniformity in religion.

4. For the administration of justice.

5. For the proportionably taxing of the people, and easy levying the same.

6. For gain by foreign commerce.

7. For husbandry, manufacture, and for arts of delight and ornament.

8. For lessening the fatigue of carriages and travelling.

9. For preventing beggars and thieves.

10. For the advancement and propagation of useful learning.

11. For increasing the people by generation.

12. For preventing the mischiefs of plagues and contagious. And withal, which of the said two states is most practicable and natural, for in these and the like particulars do lie the tests and touchstones of all proposals that can be made for the public good.

First, as to practicable, we say, that although our said extravagant proposals are both in nature possible, yet it is not obvious to every man to conceive how London, now seven times bigger than in the beginning of Queen Elizabeth's reign, should be seven times bigger than now it is, and forty-nine times bigger than A.D. 1560. To which I say, 1. That the present city of London stands upon less than 2,500 acres of ground, wherefore a city seven times as large may stand upon 10,500 acres, which is about equivalent to a circle of four miles and a half in diameter, and less than fifteen miles in circumference. 2. That a circle of ground of thirty-five miles semidiameter will bear corn, garden-stuff, fruits, hay, and timber, for the 4,690,000 inhabitants of the said city and circle, so as nothing of that kind need be brought from above thirty-five miles distance from the said city; for the number of acres within the said circle, reckoning two acres sufficient to furnish bread and drink- corn for every head, and two acres will furnish hay for every necessary horse; and that the trees which may grow in the hedgerows of the fields within the said circle may furnish timber for 600,000 houses. 3. That all live cattle and great animals can bring themselves to the said city; and that fish can be brought from the Land's End and Berwick as easily as now. 4. Of coals there is no doubt: and for water, 20s. per family (or 600,000 pounds per annum in the whole) will serve this city, especially with the help of the New River. But if by practicable be understood that the present state may be suddenly changed into either of the two above-mentioned proposals, I think it is not practicable. Wherefore the true question is, unto or towards which of the said two extravagant states it is best to bend the present state by degrees, viz., Whether it be best to lessen or enlarge the present city? In order whereunto, we inquire (as to the first question) which state is most defensible against foreign powers, saying, that if the above- mentioned housing, and a border of ground, of three-quarters of a mile broad, were encompassed with a wall and ditch of twenty miles about (as strong as any in Europe, which would cost but a million, or about a penny in the shilling of the house-rent for one year) what foreign prince could bring an army from beyond seas, able to beat--1. Our sea-forces, and next with horse harassed at sea, to resist all the fresh horse that England could make, and then conquer above a million of men, well united, disciplined, and guarded within such a wall, distant everywhere three-quarters of a mile from the housing, to elude the granadoes and great shot of the enemy? 2. As to intestine parties and factions, I suppose that 4,690,000 people united within this great city could easily govern half the said number scattered without it, and that a few men in arms within the said city and wall could also easily govern the rest unarmed, or armed in such a manner as the Sovereign shall think fit. 3. As to uniformity in religion, I conceive, that if St. Martin's parish (may as it doth) consist of about 40,000 souls, that this great city also may as well be made but as one parish, with seven times 130 chapels, in which might not only be an uniformity of common prayer, but in preaching also; for that a thousand copies of one judiciously and authentically composed sermon might be every week read in each of the said chapels without any subsequent repetition of the same, as in the case of homilies. Whereas in England (wherein are near 10,000 parishes, in each of which upon Sundays, holy days, and other extraordinary occasions there should be about 100 sermons annum, making about a million of sermons per annum in the whole) it were a miracle, if a million of sermons composed by so many men, and of so many minds and methods, should produce uniformity upon the discomposed understandings of about 8,000,000 of hearers.

4. As to the administration of justice. If in this great city shall dwell the owners of all the lands, and other valuable things in England; if within it shall be all the traders, and all the courts, offices, records, juries, and witnesses; then it follows that justice may be done with speed and ease.

5. As to the equality and easy levying of taxes. It is too certain that London hath at some time paid near half the excise of England, and that the people pay thrice as much for the hearths in London as those in the country, in proportion to the people of each, and that the charge of collecting these duties have been about a sixth part of the duty itself. Now in this great city the excise alone according to the present laws would not only be double to the whole kingdom, but also more equal. And the duty of hearths of the said city would exceed the present proceed of the whole kingdom. And as for the customs we mention them not at present.

6. Whether more would be gained by foreign commerce? The gain which England makes by lead, coals, the freight of shipping, &c., may be the same, for aught I see, in both cases. But the gain which is made by manufactures will be greater as the manufacture itself is greater and better. For in so vast a city manufactures will beget one another, and each manufacture will be divided into as many parts as possible, whereby the work of each artisan will be simple and easy. As, for example, in the making of a watch, if one man shall make the wheels, another the spring, another shall engrave the dial- plate, and another shall make the cases, then the watch will be better and cheaper than if the whole work be put upon any one man. And we also see that in towns, and in the streets of a great town, where all the inhabitants are almost of one trade, the commodity peculiar to those places is made better and cheaper than elsewhere. Moreover, when all sorts of manufactures are made in one place, there every ship that goeth forth can suddenly have its loading of so many several particulars and species as the port whereunto she is bound can take off.

Again, when the several manufactures are made in one place, and shipped off in another, the carriage, postage, and travelling charges, will enhance the price of such manufacture, and lessen the gain upon foreign commerce. And lastly, when the imported goods are spent in the port itself, where they are landed, the carriage of the same into other places will create no further charge upon such commodity; all which particulars tend to the greater gain by foreign commerce.

7. As for arts of delight and ornament. They are best promoted by the greatest number of emulators. And it is more likely that one ingenious curious man may rather be found out amongst 4,000,000 than 400 persons. But as for husbandry, viz., tillage and pasturage, I see no reason, but the second state (when each family is charged with the culture of about twenty-four acres) will best promote the same.

8. As for lessening the fatigue of carriage and travelling.

The thing speaks for itself, for if all the men of business, and all artisans, do live within five miles of each other, and if those who live without the great city do spend only such commodities as grow where they live, then the charge of carriage and travelling could be little.

9. As to the preventing of beggars and thieves.

I do not find how the differences of the said two states should make much difference in this particular; for impotents (which are but one in about 600) ought to be maintained by the rest. 2. Those who are unable to work, through the evil education of their parents, ought (for aught I know) to be maintained by their nearest kindred, as a just punishment upon them. 3. And those who cannot find work (though able and willing to perform it), by reason of the unequal application of hands to lands, ought to be provided for by the magistrate and landlord till that can be done; for there need be no beggars in countries where there are many acres of unimproved improvable land to every head, as there are in England. As for thieves, they are for the most part begotten from the same cause; for it is against Nature that any man should venture his life, limb, or liberty, for a wretched livelihood, whereas moderate labour will produce a better. But of this see Sir Thomas More, in the first part of his "Utopia."

10. As to the propagation and improvement of useful learning.

The same may be said concerning it as was above said concerning manufactures, and the arts of delight and ornaments; for in the great vast city there can be no so odd a conceit or design whereunto some assistance may not be found, which in the thin, scattered way of habitation may not be.

11. As for the increase of people by generation. I see no great difference from either of the two states, for the same may be hindered or promoted in either from the same causes.

12. As to the plague.

It is to be remembered that one time with another a plague happeneth in London once in twenty years, or thereabouts; for in the last hundred years, between the years 1582 and 1682, there have been five great plagues--viz., A.D. 1592, 1603, 1625, 1636, and 1665. And it is also to be remembered that the plagues of London do commonly kill one-fifth part of the inhabitants. Now if the whole people of England do double but in 360 years, then the annual increase of the same is but 20,000, and in twenty years 400,000. But if in the city of London there should be 2,000,000 of people (as there will be about sixty years hence), then the plague (killing one-fifth of them, namely, 400,000 once in twenty years) will destroy as many in one year as the whole nation can re-furnish in twenty; and consequently the people of the nation shall never increase. But if the people of London shall be above 4,000,000 (as in the first of our two extravagant suppositions is premised), then the people of the whole nation shall lessen above 20,000 per annum. So as if people be worth 70 pounds per head (as hath elsewhere been shown), then the said greatness of the city will be a damage to itself and the whole nation of 1,400,000 pounds per annum, and so pro rata for a greater or lesser number; wherefore to determine which of the two states is best--that is to say, towards which of the said two states authority should bend the present state, a just balance ought to be made between the disadvantages from the plague, with the advantages accruing from the other particulars above mentioned, unto which balance a more exact account of the people, and a better rule for the measure of its growth is necessary than what we have here given, or are yet able to lay down.

POSTSCRIPT.

It was not very pertinent to a discourse concerning the growth of the city of London to thrust in considerations of the time when the whole world will be fully peopled; and how to justify the Scriptures concerning the number of people mentioned in them; and concerning the number of the quick and the dead that may rise at the last day, &c. Nevertheless, since some friends, liking the said digressions and impertinences (perhaps as sauce to a dry discourse) have desired that the same might be explained and made out, I, therefore, say as followeth:-

1. If the number of acres in the habitable part of the earth be under 50,000,000,000; if 20,000,000,000 of people are more than the said number of acres will feed (few or no countries being so fully peopled), and for that in six doublings (which will be in 2,000 years) the present 320,000,000 will exceed the said 20,000,000,000.

2. That the number of all those who have died since the Flood is the sum of all the products made by multiplying the number of the doubling periods mentioned in the first column of the last table, by the number of people respectively affixed to them in the third column of the same table, the said sum being divided by 40 (one dying out of 40 per annum out of the whole mass of mankind), which quotient is 12,570,000,000; whereunto may be added, for those that died before the Flood, enough to make the last-mentioned number 20,000,000,000, as the full number of all that died from the beginning of the world to the year 1682, unto which, if 320,000,000, the number of those who are now alive, be added, the total of the quick and the dead will amount but

unto one fifth part of the graves which the surface of Ireland will afford, without ever putting two bodies into any one grave; for there be in Ireland 28,000 square English miles, each whereof will afford about 4,000,000 of graves, and consequently above 114,000,000,000 of graves, viz., about five times the number of the quick and the dead which should arise at the last day, in case the same had been in the year 1682.

3. Now, if there may be place for five times as many graves in Ireland as are sufficient for all that ever died, and if the earth of one grave weigh five times as much as the body interred therein, then a turf less than a foot thick pared off from a fifth part of the surface of Ireland, will be equivalent in bulk and weight to all the bodies that ever were buried, and may serve as well for that purpose as the two mountains aforementioned in the body of this discourse. From all which it is plain how madly they were mistaken who did so petulantly vilify what the Holy Scriptures have delivered.

FURTHER OBSERVATION UPON THE DUBLIN BILLS; Or, Accounts of the Houses, Hearths, Baptisms, and Burials in that City.

THE STATIONER TO THE READER.

I have not thought fit to make any alteration of the first edition, but have only added a new table, with observation upon it, placing the same in the front of what was before, which, perhaps, might have been as well placed after the like table at the eighth page of the first edition.

DUBLIN, 1682.

Parishes Houses Fireplaces Baptised Buried St. James's 272 836 } St. Katherine's 540 2,198 } 122 306 St. Nicholas } Without and } 1,064 4,082 145 414 St. Patrick's } St. Bridget's 395 1,903 68 149 St. Audone's 276 1,510 56 164 St. Michael's 174 884 34 50 St. John's 302 1,636 74 101 St. Nicholas } Within and } 153 902 26 52 Christ Church Lib. } St. Warburgh's 240 1,638 45 105 St. Michan's 938 3,516 124 389 St. Andrew's 864 3,638 131 300 St.

Kevin's 554 2,120 } 87 233 Donnybrook 253 506 } 6,025 25,369 912 2,263

The table hath been made for the year 1682, wherein is to be noted -

1. That the houses which A.D. 1671 were but 3,850 are, A.D. 1682, 6,025; but whether this difference is caused by the real increase of housing, or by fraud and defect in the former accounts, is left to consideration. For the burials of people have increased but from 1,696 to 2,263, according to which proportion the 3,850 houses A.D. 1671 should A.D. 1682 have been but 5,143, wherefore some fault may be suspected as aforesaid, when farming the hearth-money was in agitation.

2. The hearths have increased according to the burials, and one- third of the said increase more, viz., the burials A.D. 1671 were 1,696, the one-third whereof is 563, which put together makes 2,259, which is near the number of burials A.D. 1682. But the hearths A.D. 1671 were 17,500, whereof the one-third is 5,833, making in all but 23,333; whereas the whole hearths A.D. 1682 were 25,369, viz., one- third and better of the said 5,833 more.

3. The housing were A.D. 1671 but 3,850, which if they had increased A.D. 1682 but according to the burials, they had been but 5,143, or, according to the hearths, had been but 5,488, whereas they appear 6,025, increasing double to the hearths. So as it is likely there hath been some error in the said account of the housing, unless the new housing be very small, and have but one chimney apiece, and that one-fourth part of them are untenanted. On the other hand, it is more likely that when 1,696 died per annum there were near 6,000; for 6,000 houses at 8 inhabitants per house, would make the number of the people to be 48,000, and the number of 1,696 that died according to the rule of one out of 30, would have made the number of inhabitants about 50,000: for which reason I continue to believe there was some error in the account of 3,850 houses as aforesaid, and the rather because there is no ground from experience to think that in eleven years the houses in Dublin have increased from 3,850 to 6,025.

Moreover, I rather think that the number of 6,025 is yet short, because that number at 8 heads per house makes the inhabitants to be but 48,200; whereas the 2,263 who died in the year 1682, according to the aforementioned rule of one dying out of 30 makes the number of people to be 67,890, the medium betwixt which number and 48,200 is 58,045, which is the best estimate I can make of that matter, which I hope authority will ere long rectify, by direct and exact inquiries.

4. As to the births, we say that A.D. 1640, 1641, and 1642, at London, just before the troubles in religion began, the births were five-sixths of the burials, by reason I suppose of the greaterness of families in London above the country, and the fewer breeders, and not for want of registering. Wherefore, deducting one-sixth of 2,263, which is 377, there remains 1,886 for the probable number of births in Dublin for the year 1682; whereas but 912 are represented to have been christened in that year, though 1,023 were christened A.D. 1671, when there died but 1,696, which decreasing of the christening, and increasing of the burials, shows the increase of non-registering in the legal books, which must be the increase of Roman Catholics at Dublin.

The scope of this whole paper therefore is, that the people of Dublin are rather 58,000 than 32,000, and that the dissenters, who do not register their baptisms, have increased from 391 to 974: but of dissenters, none have increased but the Roman Catholics, whose numbers have increased from about two to five in the said years. The exacter knowledge whereof may also be better had from direct inquiries.

OBSERVATIONS UPON THE DUBLIN BILLS OF MORTALITY, 1681: AND THE STATE OF THAT CITY.

The observations upon the London bills of mortality have been a new light to the world, and the like observation upon those of Dublin may serve as snuffers to make the same candle burn clearer.

The London observations flowed from bills regularly kept for near one hundred years, but these are squeezed out of six straggling London bills, out of fifteen Dublin bills, and from a note of the families and hearths in each parish of Dublin, which are all digested into the one table or sheet annexed, consisting of three parts, marked A, B, C; being indeed the A, B, C of public economy, and even of that policy which tends to peace and plenty.

Observations upon the Table A.

1. The total of the burials in London (for the said six straggling years mentioned in the Table A) is 120,170, whereof the medium or sixth part is 20,028, and exceeds the burials of Paris, as may appear by the late bills of that city.

2. The births, for the same time, are 73,683, the medium or sixth part whereof is 12,280, which is about five-eighth parts of the burials, and shows that London would in time decrease quite away, were it not supplied out of the country, where are about five births for four burials, the proportion of breeders in the country being greater than in the city.

3. The burials in Dublin for the said six years were 9,865, the sixth part or medium whereof is 1,644, which is about the twelfth part of the London burials, and about a fifth part over. So as the people of London do hereby seem to be above twelve times as many as those of Dublin.

4. The births in the same time at Dublin are 6,157, the sixth part or medium whereof is 1,026, which is also about five-eighth parts of the 1,644 burials, which shows that the proportion between burials and births are alike at London and Dublin, and that the accounts are kept alike, and consequently are likely to be true, there being no confederacy for that purpose; which, if they be true, we then say -

5. That the births are the best way (till the accounts of the people shall be purposely taken) whereby to judge of the increase and decrease of people, that of burials being subject to more contingencies and variety of causes.

6. If births be as yet the measure of the people, and that the births (as has been shown) are as five to eight, then eight-fifths of the births is the number of the burials, where the year was not considerable for extraordinary sickness or salubrity, and is the rule whereby to measure the same. As for example, the medium of births in Dublin was 1,026, the eight-fifths whereof is 1,641, but the real burials were 1,644; so as in the said years they differed little from the 1,641, which was the standard of health, and consequently the years 1680, 1674, and 1668 were sickly years, more or less, as they exceeded the said number, 1,641; and the rest were healthful years, more or less, as they fell short of the same number. But the city was more or less populous, as the births differed from the number 1,026, viz., populous in the years 1680, 1679, 1678, and 1668, for other causes of this difference in births are very occult and uncertain.

7. What hath been said of Dublin, serves also for London.

8. It hath already been observed by the London bills that there are more males than females. It is to be further noted, that in these six London bills, also, there is not one instance either in the births or burials to the contrary.

9. It hath been formerly observed that in the years wherein most die fewest are born, and vice versa. The same may be further observed in males and females, viz., when fewest males are born then most die: for here the males died as twelve to eleven, which is above the mean proportion of fourteen to thirteen, but were born but as nineteen to eighteen, which is below the same.

Observations upon the Table B.

1. From the Table B it appears that the medium of the fifteen years' burials (being 24,199) is 1,613, whereas the medium of the other six years in the Table A was 1,644, and that the medium of the fifteen years' births (being in all 14,765) is 984, whereas the medium of the said other six years was 1,026. That is to say, there were both fewer births and burials in these fifteen years

than in the other six years, which is a probable sign that at a medium there were fewer people also.

2. The medium of births for the fifteen years being 984, whereof eight-fifths (being 1,576) is the standard of health for the said fifteen years; and the triple of the said 1,576 being 4,728, is the standard for each of the ternaries of the fifteen years within the said table.

3. That 2,952, the triple of 984 births, is for each ternary the standard of people's increase and decrease from the year 1666 to 1680 inclusive, viz., the people increased in the second ternary, and decreased from the same in the third and fourth ternaries, but re-increased in the fifth ternary beyond any other.

4. That the last ternary was withal very healthful, the burials being but 4,624, viz., below 4,728, the standard\

5. That according to this proportion of increase, the housing of Dublin have probably increased also.

Observations upon the Table C.

1. First, from the Table C it appears, 1. That the housing of Dublin is such, as that there are not five hearths in each house one with another, but nearer five than four.

2. That in St. Warburgh's parish are near six hearths to a house. In St. John's five. In St. Michael's above five. In St. Nicholas Within above six. In Christ Church above seven. In St. James's and St. Katherine's, and in St. Michan's, not four. In St. Kevin's about four.

3. That in St. James's, St. Michan's, St. Bride's, St. Warburgh's, St. Andrew's, St. Michael's, and St. Patrick's, all the christenings were but 550, and the burials 1,055, viz., near double; and that in the rest of the parishes the christenings were five, and the burials seven, viz., as 457 to 634. Now whether

the cause of this difference was negligence in accounts, or the greaterness of the families, &c., is worth inquiring.

4. It is hard to say in what order (as to greatness) these parishes ought to stand, some having most families, some most hearths, some most births, and others most burials. Some parishes exceeding the rest in two, others in three of the said four particulars, but none in all four. Wherefore this table ranketh them according to the plurality of the said four particulars wherein each excelleth the other.

5. The London observations reckon eight heads in each family, according to which estimation, there are 32,000 souls in the 4,000 families of Dublin, which is but half of what most men imagine, of which but about one sixth part are able to bear arms, besides the royal regiment.

6. Without the knowledge of the true number of people, as a principle, the whole scope and use of the keeping bills of births and burials is impaired; wherefore by laborious conjectures and calculations to deduce the number of people from the births and burials, may be ingenious, but very preposterous.

7. If the number of families in Dublin be about 4,000, then ten men in one week (at the charge of about 5 pounds surveying eight families in an hour) may directly, and without algebra, make an account of the whole people, expressing their several ages, sex, marriages, title, trade, religion, &c., and those who survey the hearths, or the constables or the parish clerks (may, if required) do the same ex officio, and without other charge, by the command of the chief governor, the diocesan, or the mayor.

8. The bills of London have since their beginning admitted several alterations and improvements, and 8 or 10 pounds per annum surcharge, would make the bills of Dublin to exceed all others, and become an excellent instrument of Government. To which purpose the forms for weekly, quarterly, and yearly bills are humbly recommended, viz.

TABLE A-- YEARLY BILLS OF MORTALITY FOR A.D. LONDON and DUBLIN. Burials Births Burials Births 1680 21,053 12,747 1,826 1,096 1679 21,730 12,288 1,397 1,061 1678 20,678 12,601 1,401 1,045 1674 21,201 11,851 2,106 942 1672 18,230 12,563 1,436 987 1668 17,278 11,633 1,699 1,026 120,170 73,683 9,865 6,157 The medium or 6th part whereof is part whereof is 20,028 12,280 1,644 1,026

TABLE A--CONTINUED

A.D. LONDON. BURIALS. BIRTHS. Male Female Male Female 1680 11,039 10,044 6,543 6,041 1679 11,154 10,576 6,247 6,041 1678 10,681 9,977 6,568 6,033 1674 11,000 10,196 6,113 5,738 1672 9,560 8,070 6,443 6,120 1668 9,111 8,167 6,073 5,566 62,545 57,030 37,992 35,697 The medium or 6th part whereof is part whereof is 10,424 9,505 6,332 5,949

TABLE B.--DUBLIN.

A.D. Burials Births In Ternaries of Years 1666 1,480 952 } 1667 1,642 1,001 } 4,821 2,979 1668 1,699 1,026 } 1669 1,666 1,000 } 1670 1,713 1,067 } 5,353 3,070 1671 1,974 1,003 } 1672 1,436 967 } 1673 1,531 933 } 5,073 2,842 1674 2,106 942 } 1675 1,578 823 } 1676 1,391 952 } 4,328 2,672 1677 1,359 897 } 1678 1,401 1,045 } 1679 1,397 1,061 } 4,624 3,202 1680 1,826 1,096 } 24,199 14,765 24,199 14,765 The medium } or 15th }1,613 984 1,613 984 part whereof } is }

TABLE C.

THE PARISHES OF DUBLIN A.D. A.D., 1670-71-72 1671. at a medium Families Hearths Births Burials St. Katherine's 661 2,399 161 290 and St. James's St. Nicholas Without 490 2,348 207 262 St. Michan's 656 2,301 127 221 St. Andrew's with Donnybrook 483 2,123 108 178 St. Bridget's 416 1,989 70 100 St. John's 244 1,337 70 138 St. Warburgh's 267 1,650 54 103 St. Audaen's 216 1,081 53 121 St. Michael's 140 793 44 59 St. Kevin's 106 433 64 133 St. Nicholas Within 93 614 28 34 St. Patrick's Liberties 52 255 21 44

Christ Church and Trinity College, per estimate 26 197 - 1 3,850 17,500 1,013 1,696

Houses built between 1671 and 1681, per estimate 150 550 4,000 18,150

A WEEKLY BILL OF MORTALITY FOR THE CITY OF DUBLIN, Ending the XXX day of XXX 1681.

PARISHES' NAMES. St. Katharine's and St. James's St. Nicholas Without St. Michan's St. Andrew's with Donnybrook St. Bridget's St. John's St. Warburgh's St. Audaen's St. Michael's St. Kevin's St. Nicholas Within St. Patrick's Liberties Christ Church and Trinity College Totals

[The columns for the table are: Births, Males, Females, Burials, Under 16 years old, Plague, Small Pox, Measles, Spotted Fever. In the book there are no figures in the table at all.--DP.]

A QUARTERLY BILL OF MORTALITY, Beginning XXX and ending XXX for the City of DUBLIN PARISHES' NAMES. St. Katharine's and St. James's St. Nicholas Without St. Michan's St. Andrew's with Donnybrook St. Bridget's St. John's St. Warburgh's St. Audaen's St. Michael's St. Kevin's St. Nicholas Within St. Patrick's Liberties Christ Church and Trinity College Totals

[The columns for the table are: Births 1.; Marriages 2.; Buried under 16 years olds; Buried above 60 years old; Measles, Spotted Fever, Small Pox, Plague; Consumption, Dropsy, Gout, Stone; Fever, Pleurisy, Quinsy, Sudden Death; Aged above 70 years old; Infants under 2 years old; All other Casualties. In the book there are no figures in the table at all.--DP.]

AN ACCOUNT OF THE PEOPLE OF DUBLIN FOR ONE YEAR, Ending the 24th of March, 1681. PARISHES' NAMES. St. Katharine's and St. James's St. Nicholas Without St. Michan's St. Andrew's with Donnybrook St. Bridget's St. John's St. Warburgh's St. Audaen's St. Michael's St. Kevin's St. Nicholas

Within St. Patrick's Liberties Christ Church and Trinity College Totals

[The columns for the table are: Number of person; Males; Females; Remarried Persons; Persons under 16 years old; Persons above 60 years old; Protestants of above 16 years old; Papists of above 16 years old; Of all other religions above 16 years old; Births; Burials; Marriages. In the book there are no figures in the table at all.--DP.]

CASUALTIES AND DISEASES. Aged above 70 years Epilepsy and planet Abortive and still-born Fever and ague Childbed women Pleurisy Convulsion Quinsy Teeth Executed, murdered, Worms drowned Gout and sciatica Plague and spotted fever Stone Griping of the guts Palsy Scouring, vomiting Consumption and French bleeding pox Small pox Dropsy and tympany Measles Rickets and livergrown Neither of all the other Headache and megrim sorts

A POSTSCRIPT TO THE STATIONER.

Whereas you complain that these observations make no sufficient bulk, I could answer you that I wish the bulk of all books were less; but do nevertheless comply with you in adding what follows, viz.:

1. That the parishes of Dublin are very unequal; some having in them above 600 families, and others under thirty.

2. That thirteen parishes are too few for 4,000 families; the middling parishes of London containing 120 families; according to which rate there should be about thirty-three parishes in Dublin.

3. It is said that there are 84,000 houses or families in London, which is twenty-one times more than are in Dublin, and yet the births and burials of London are but twelve times those of Dublin, which shows that the inhabitants of Dublin are more crowded and straitened in their housing than those of London; and consequently that to increase the buildings of Dublin will make

that city more conformable to London.

4. I shall also add some reasons for altering the present forms of the Dublin bills of mortality, according to what hath been here recommended--viz.:

1. We give the distinctions of males and females in the births only; for that the burials must, at one time or another, be in the same proportion with the births.

2. We do in the weekly and quarterly bills propose that notice be taken in the burials of what numbers die above sixty and seventy, and what under sixteen, six, and two years old, foreseeing good uses to be made of that distinction.

3. We do in the yearly bill reduce the casualties to about twenty- four, being such as may be discerned by common sense, and without art, conceiving that more will but perplex and imbroil the account. And in the quarterly bills we reduce the diseases to three heads-- viz., contagious, acute, and chronical, applying this distinction to parishes, in order to know how the different situation, soil, and way of living in each parish doth dispose men to each of the said three species; and in the weekly bills we take notice not only of the plague, but of the other contagious diseases in each parish, that strangers and fearful persons may thereby know how to dispose of themselves.

4. We mention the number of the people, as the fundamental term in all our proportions; and without which all the rest will be almost fruitless.

5. We mention the number of marriages made in every quarter, and in every year, as also the proportion which married persons bear to the whole, expecting in such observations to read the improvement of the nation.

6. As for religions, we reduce them to three--viz.: (1) those who have the Pope of Rome for their head; (2) who are governed by the laws of their country; (3) those who rely respectively upon their own private judgments. Now, whether these distinctions should be taken notice of or not, we do but

faintly recommend, seeing many reasons pro and con for the same; and, therefore, although we have mentioned it as a matter fit to be considered, yet we humbly leave it to authority.

TWO ESSAYS IN POLITICAL ARITHMETIC, Concerning the People, Housing, Hospitals, &c., of London and Paris.

TO THE KING'S MOST EXCELLENT MAJESTY.

I do presume, in a very small paper, to show your Majesty that your City of London seems more considerable than the two best cities of the French monarchy, and for aught I can find, greater than any other of the universe, which because I can say without flattery, and by such demonstration as your Majesty can examine, I humbly pray your Majesty to accept from

Your Majesty's Most humble, loyal, and obedient subject, WILLIAM PETTY.

AN ESSAY IN POLITICAL ARITHMETIC

Tending to prove that London hath more people and housing than the cities of Paris and Rouen put together, and is also more considerable in several other respects.

1. The medium of the burials at London in the three last years-- viz., 1683, 1684, and 1685, wherein there was no extraordinary sickness, and wherein the christenings do correspond in their ordinary proportions with the burials and christenings of each year one with another, was 22,337, and the like medium of burials for the three last Paris bills we could procure--viz., for the years 1682, 1683, and 1684 (whereof the last as appears by the christenings to have been very sickly), is 19,887.

2. The city of Bristol in England appears to be by good estimate of its trade

and customs as great as Rouen in France, and the city of Dublin in Ireland appears to have more chimneys than Bristol, and consequently more people, and the burials in Dublin were, A.D. 1682 (being a sickly year) but 2,263.

3. Now the burials of Paris (being 19,887) being added to the burials of Dublin (supposed more than at Rouen) being 2,263, makes but 22,150, whereas the burials of London were 187 more, or 22,337, or as about 6 to 7.

4. If those who die unnecessarily, and by miscarriage in L'Hotel Dieu in Paris (being above 3,000), as hath been elsewhere shown, or any part thereof, should be subtracted out of the Paris burials aforementioned, then our assertion will be stronger, and more proportionable to what follows concerning the housing of those cities, viz.:

5. There were burnt at London, A.D. 1666, above 13,000 houses, which being but a fifth part of the whole, the whole number of houses in the said year were above 65,000; and whereas the ordinary burials of London have increased between the years 1666 and 1686, above one-third the total of the houses at London, A.D. 1686, must be about 87,000, which A.D. 1682, appeared by account to have been 84,000.

6. Monsieur Moreri, the great French author of the late geographical dictionaries, who makes Paris the greatest city in the world, doth reckon but 50,000 houses in the same, and other authors and knowing men much less; nor are there full 7,000 houses in the city of Dublin, so as if the 50,000 houses of Paris, and the 7,000 houses in the city of Dublin were added together, the total is but 57,000 houses, whereas those of London are 87,000 as aforesaid, or as 6 to 9.

7. As for the shipping and foreign commerce of London, the common sense of all men doth judge it to be far greater than that of Paris and Rouen put together.

8. As to the wealth and gain accruing to the inhabitants of London and Paris

by law-suits (or La chicane) I only say that the courts of London extend to all England and Wales, and affect seven millions of people, whereas those of Paris do not extend near so far. Moreover, there is no palpable conspicuous argument at Paris for the number and wealth of lawyers like the buildings and chambers in the two Temples, Lincoln's Inn, Gray's Inn, Doctors' Commons, and the seven other inns in which are chimneys, which are to be seen at London, besides many lodgings, halls, and offices, relating to the same.

9. As to the plentiful and easy living of the people we say,

(a.) That the people of Paris to those of London, being as about 6 to 7, and the housing of the same as about 6 to 9, we infer that the people do not live at London so close and crowded as at Paris, but can afford themselves more room and liberty.

(b.) That at London the hospitals are better and more desirable than those of Paris, for that in the best at Paris there die two out of fifteen, whereas at London there die out of the worst scarce 2 out of 16, and yet but a fiftieth part of the whole die out of the hospitals at London, and two-fifths, or twenty times that proportion die out of the Paris hospitals which are of the same kind; that is to say, the number of those at London, who choose to lie sick in hospitals rather than in their own houses, are to the like people of Paris as one to twenty; which shows the greater poverty or want of means in the people of Paris than those of London.

(c.) We infer from the premises, viz., the dying scarce two of sixteen out of the London hospitals, and about two of fifteen in the best of Paris, to say nothing of L'Hotel Dieu, that either the physicians and chirurgeons of London are better than those of Paris, or that the air of London is more wholesome.

10. As for the other great cities of the world, if Paris were the greatest we need say no more in behalf of London. As for Pekin in China, we have no account fit to reason upon; nor is there anything in the description of the two late voyages of the Chinese emperor from that city into East and West Tartary,

in the years 1682 and 1683, which can make us recant what we have said concerning London. As for Delhi and Agra, belonging to the Mogul, we find nothing against our position, but much to show the vast numbers which attend that emperor in his business and pleasures.

11. We shall conclude with Constantinople and Grand Cairo; as for Constantinople it hath been said by one who endeavoured to show the greatness of that city, and the greatness of the plague which raged in it, that there died 1,500 per diem, without other circumstances; to which we answer, that in the year 1665 there died in London 1,200 per diem, and it hath been well proved that the Plague of London never carried away above one-fifth of the people, whereas it is commonly believed that in Constantinople, and other eastern cities, and even in Italy and Spain, that the plague takes away two-fifths, one half, or more; wherefore where 1,200 is but one-fifth of the people it is probable that the number was greater, than where 1,500 was two-fifths or one half, &c.

12. As for Grand Cairo it is reported, that 73,000 died in ten weeks, or 1,000 per diem, where note, that at Grand Cairo the plague comes and goes away suddenly, and that the plague takes away two or three-fifths parts of the people as aforesaid; so as 73,000 was probably the number of those that died of the plague in one whole year at Grand Cairo, whereas at London, A.D. 1665, 97,000 were brought to account to have died in that year. Wherefore it is certain, that that city wherein 97,000 was but one-fifth of the people, the number was greater than where 73,000 was two-fifths or the half.

We therefore conclude, that London hath more people, housing, shipping, and wealth, than Paris and Rouen put together; and for aught yet appears, is more considerable than any other city in the universe, which was propounded to be proved.

AN ESSAY IN POLITICAL ARITHMETIC

Tending to prove that in the hospital called L'Hotel Dieu at Paris, there die above 3,000 per annum by reason of ill accommodation.

1. It appears that A.D. 1678 there entered into the Hospital of La Charite 2,647 souls, of which there died there within the said year 338, which is above an eighth part of the said 2,647; and that in the same year there entered into L'Hotel Dieu 21,491, and that there died out of that number 5,630, which is above one quarter, so as about half the said 5,630, being 2,815, seem to have died for want of as good usage and accommodation as might have been had at La Charite.

2. Moreover, in the year 1679 there entered into La Charite 3,118, of which there died 452, which is above a seventh part, and in the same year there entered into L'Hotel Dieu 28,635, of which there died 8,397; and in both the said years 1678 and 1679 (being very different in their degrees of mortality) there entered into L'Hotel Dieu 28,635 and 21,491--in all 50,126, the medium whereof is 25,063; and there died out of the same in the said two years, 5,630 and 8,397--in all 14,027, the medium whereof is 7,013.

3. There entered in the said years into La Charite 2,647 and 3,118, in all 5,765, the medium whereof is 2,882, whereof there died 338 and 452, in all 790, the medium whereof is 395.

4. Now, if there died out of L'Hotel Dieu 7,013 per annum, and that the proportion of those that died out of L'Hotel Dieu is double to those that died out of La Charite (as by the above numbers it appears to be near thereabouts), then it follows that half the said numbers of 7,013, being 3,506, did not die by natural necessity, but by the evil administration of that hospital.

5. This conclusion seemed at the first sight very strange, and rather to be some mistake or chance than a solid and real truth; but considering the same matter as it appeared at London, we were more reconciled to the belief of it, viz.:-

(a.) In the Hospital of St. Bartholomew in London, there was sent out and cured in the year 1685, 1,764 persons, and there died out of the said hospital 252. Moreover, there were sent out and cured out of St. Thomas's Hospital 1,523, and buried, 209--that is to say, there were cured in both hospitals 3,287, and buried out of both hospitals 461, and consequently cured and buried 3,748, of which number the 461 buried is less than an eighth part; whereas at La Charite the part that died was more than an eighth part; which shows that out of the most poor and wretched hospitals of London there died fewer in proportion than out of the best in Paris.

(b.) Furthermore, it hath been above shown that there died out of La Charite at a medium 395 per annum, and 141 out of Les Incurables, making in all 536; and that out of St. Bartholomew's and St. Thomas's Hospitals, London, there died at a medium but 461, of which Les Incurables are part; which shows that although there be more people in London than in Paris, yet there went at London not so many people to hospitals as there did at Paris, although the poorest hospitals at London were better than the best at Paris; which shows that the poorest people at London have better accommodation in their own houses than the best hospital of Paris affordeth.

6. Having proved that there die about 3,506 persons at Paris unnecessarily, to the damage of France, we come next to compute the value of the said damage, and of the remedy thereof, as follows, viz., the value of the said 3,506 at 60 livres sterling per head, being about the value of Argier slaves (which is less than the intrinsic value of people at Paris), the whole loss of the subjects of France in that hospital seems to be 60 times 3,506 livres sterling per annum, viz., 210,360 livres sterling, equivalent to about 2,524,320 French livres.

7. It hath appeared that there came into L'Hotel Dieu at a medium 25,063 per annum, or 2,089 per mensem, and that the whole stock of what remained in the precedent months is at a medium about 2,108 (as may appear by the third line of the Table No. 5, which shall be shortly published), viz., the medium of months is 2,410 for the sickly year 1679, whereunto 1,806 being added as the medium of months for the year 1678, makes 4,216, the medium whereof is the 2,108 above mentioned; which number being added to the 2,089 which entered

each month, makes 4,197 for the number of sick which are supposed to be always in L'Hotel Dieu one time with another.

8. Now, if 60 French livres per annum for each of the said 4,197 sick persons were added to the present ordinary expense of that hospital (amounting to an addition of 251,820 livres), it seems that so many lives might be saved as are worth above ten times that sum, and this by doing a manifest deed of charity to mankind.

Memorandum.--That A.D. 1685, the burials of London were 23,222, and those of Amsterdam 6,245; from whence, and the difference of air, it is probable that the people of London are quadruple to those of Amsterdam.

OBSERVATIONS UPON THE CITIES OF LONDON AND ROME

1. That before the year 1630 the christenings at London exceeded the burials of the same, but about the year 1655 they were scarce half; and now about two-thirds.

2. Before the restoration of monarchy in England, A.D. 1660, the people of Paris were more than those of London and Dublin put together, whereas now, the people of London are more than those of Paris and Rome, or of Paris and Rouen.

3. A.D. 1665 one fifth part of the then people of London, or 97,000, died of the plague, and in the next year, 1666, 13,000 houses, or one fifth part of all the housing of London, were burnt also.

4. At the birth of Christ old Rome was the greatest city of the world, and London the greatest at the coronation of King James II., and near six times as great as the present Rome, wherein are 119,000 souls besides Jews.

5. In the years of King Charles II.'s death, and King James II.'s coronation (which were neither of them remarkable for extraordinary sickliness or

healthfulness) the burials did wonderfully agree, viz., A.D. 1684, they were 23,202, and A.D. 1685, they were 23,222, the medium whereof is 23,212. And the christenings did very wonderfully agree also, having been A.D. 1684, 14,702, and A.D. 1685, 14,732, the medium whereof is 14,716, which consistence was never seen before, the said number of 23,212 burials making the people of London to be 696,360, at the rate of one dying per annum out of 30.

6. Since the great Fire of London, A.D. 1666, about 7 parts of 15 of the present vast city hath been new built, and is with its people increased near one half, and become equal to Paris and Rome put together, the one being the seat of the great French Monarchy, and the other of the Papacy.

FIVE ESSAYS IN POLITICAL ARITHMETIC

I. Objections from the city of Ray in Persia, and from Monsier Auzout, against two former essays, answered, and that London hath as many people as Paris, Rome, and Rouen put together.

II. A comparison between London and Paris in 14 particulars.

III. Proofs that at London, within its 134 parishes named in the bills of mortality, there live about 696,000 people.

IV. An estimate of the people in London, Paris, Amsterdam, Venice, Rome, Dublin, Bristol, and Rouen, with several observations upon the same.

V. Concerning Holland and the rest of the Seven United Provinces.

TO THE KING'S MOST EXCELLENT MAJESTY

Sir,

Your Majesty having graciously accepted my two late essays, about the cities and hospitals of London and Paris, as also my observations on Rome and Rouen; I do (after six months' waiting for what may be said against my several doctrines by the able men of Europe) humbly present your Majesty with a few other papers upon the same subject, to strengthen, explain, and enlarge the former; hoping by such real arguments, better to praise and magnify your Majesty, than by any other the most specious words and eulogies that can be imagined by

Your Majesty's Most humble, loyal And obedient subject, WILLIAM PETTY.

THE FIRST ESSAY.

It could not be expected that an assertion of London's being bigger than Paris and Rouen, or than Paris and Rome put together, and bigger than any city of the world, should escape uncontradicted; and 'tis also expected that I (if continuing in the same persuasion), should make some reply to those contradictions. In order whereunto,

I begin with the ingenious author of the "Republique des Lettres," who saith that Rey in Persia is far bigger than London, for that in the sixth century of Christianity (I suppose, A.D. 550 the middle of that century), it had 15,000, or rather 44,000 mosques or Mahometan temples; to which I reply, that I hope this objector is but in jest, for that Mahomet was not born till about the year 570, and had no mosques till about 50 years after.

In the next place I reply to the excellent Monsieur Auzout's "Letters from Rome," who is content that London, Westminster, and Southwark may have as many people as Paris and its suburbs; and but faintly denieth, that all the housing within the bills may have almost as many people as Paris and Rouen, but saith that several parishes inserted into these bills are distant from, and not contiguous with London, and that Grant so understood it.

To which (as his main if not his only objection) we answer: --(l) That the

London bills appear in Grant's book to have been always, since the year 1636; as they now are; (2) That about fifty years since, three or four parishes, formerly somewhat distant, were joined by interposed buildings to the bulk of the city, and therefore then inserted into the bills; (3) That since fifty years the whole buildings being more than double have perfected that union, so as there is no house within the said bills from which one may not call to some other house; (4) All this is confirmed by authority of the king and city, and the custom of fifty years; (5) That there are but three parishes under any colour of this exception which are scarce one-fifty-second part of the whole.

Upon the whole matter, upon sight of Monsieur Auzout's large letter, dated the 19th of November, from Rome, I made remarks upon every paragraph thereof, but suppressing it (because it looked like a war against a worthy person with whom I intended none, whereas, in truth, it was but a reconciling explication of some doubts) I have chosen the shorter and softer way of answering Monsieur Auzout as followeth, viz.:-

Concerning the number of people in London, as also in Paris, Rouen, and Rome, viz.:-

Monsieur Auzout allegeth an authentic account that there are 23,223 houses in Paris, wherein do live about eighty thousand families, and therefore supposing three and a half families to live in every of the said houses, one with another, the number of families will be 81,280; and Monsier Auzout also allowing six heads to each family, the utmost number of people in Paris, according to that opinion, will be 487,680.

The medium of the Paris burials was not denied by Monsier Auzout to be 19,887, nor that there died 3,506 unnecessarily out of the L'Hotel Dieu; wherefore deducting the said last number out of the former, the net standard for burials at Paris will be 16,381, so, as the number of people there, allowing but one to die out of thirty (which is more advantageous to Paris than Monsieur Auzout's opinion of one to die out of twenty-five) the number of people at Paris will be 491,430 more than by Monsieur Auzout's own last-mentioned account 491,430.

And the medium of the said two Paris accounts is 488,055.

The medium of the London burials is really 23,212, which, multiplied by thirty (as hath been done for Paris), the number of the people there will be 696,360.

The number of houses at London appears by the register to be 105,315, whereunto adding one-tenth part of the same, or 10,315, as the least number of double families that can be supposed in London, the total of families will be 115,840, and allowing six heads for each family, as was done for Paris, the total of the people at London will be 695,076.

The medium of the two last London accounts is 695,718.

So, as the people of Paris, according to the above account, is 488,055. Of Rouen, according to Monsieur Auzout's utmost demands 80,000. Of Rome, according to his own report thereof in a former letter 125,000. Total 693,055.

So as there are more people at London than at Paris, Rouen, and Rome by 2,663.

Memorandum.--That the parishes of Islington, Newington, and Hackney, for which only there is any colour of non-contiguity, is not one- fifty-second part of what is contained in the bills of mortality, and consequently London, without the said three parishes, hath more people than Paris and Rouen put together, by 114,284.

Which number of 114,284 is probably more people than any other city of France contains.

THE SECOND ESSAY.

As for other comparisons of London with Paris, we farther repeat and enlarge what hath been formerly said upon those matters, as followeth, viz.:-

1. That forty per cent. die out of the hospitals at Paris where so many die unnecessarily, and scarce one-twentieth of that proportion out of the hospitals of London, which have been shown to be better than the best of Paris.

2. That at Paris 81,280 kitchens are within less than 24,000 street-doors, which makes less cleanly and convenient way of living than at London.

3. Where the number of christenings are near unto, or exceed the burials, the people are poorer, having few servants and little equipage.

4. The river Thames is more pleasant and navigable than the Seine, and its waters better and more wholesome; and the bridge of London is the most considerable of all Europe.

5. The shipping and foreign trade of London is incomparably greater than that at Paris and Rouen.

6. The lawyers' chambers at London have 2,772 chimnies in them, and are worth 140,000 pounds sterling, or 3,000,000 of French livres, besides the dwellings of their families elsewhere.

7. The air is more wholesome, for that at London scarce two of sixteen die out of the worst hospitals, but at Paris above two of fifteen out of the best. Moreover the burials of Paris are one- fifth part above and below the medium, but at London not above one- twelfth, so as the intemperies of the air at Paris is far greater than at London.

8. The fuel cheaper, and lies in less room, the coals being a wholesome sulphurous bitumen.

9. All the most necessary sorts of victuals, and of fish, are cheaper, and

drinks of all sorts in greater variety and plenty.

10. The churches of London we leave to be judged by thinking that nothing at Paris is so great as St. Paul's was, and is like to be, nor so beautiful as Henry the Seventh's chapel.

11. On the other hand, it is probable, that there is more money in Paris than London, if the public revenue (grossly speaking, quadruple to that of England) be lodged there.

12. Paris hath not been for these last fifty years so much infested with the plague as London; now that at London the plague (which between the years 1591 and 1666 made five returns, viz., every fifteen years, at a medium, and at each time carried away one-fifth of the people) hath not been known for the 21 years last past, and there is a visible way by God's ordinary blessing to lessen the same by two-thirds when it next appeareth.

13. As to the ground upon which Paris stands in respect of London, we say, that if there be five stories or floors of housing at Paris, for four at London, or in that proportion, then the 82,000 families of Paris stand upon the equivalent of 65,000 London housteds, and if there be 115,000 families at London, and but 82,000 at Paris, then the proportion of the London ground to that of Paris is as 115 to sixty-five, or as twenty-three to thirteen.

14. Moreover Paris is said to be an oval of three English miles long and two and a half broad, the area whereof contains but five and a half square miles; but London is seven miles long, and one and a quarter broad at a medium, which makes an area of near nine square miles, which proportion of five and half to nine differs little from that of thirteen to twenty-three.

15. Memorandum, that in Nero's time, as Monsieur Chivreau reporteth, there died 300,000 people of the plague in old Rome; now if there died three of ten then and there, being a hotter country, as there dies two of ten at London, the number of people at that time, was but a million, whereas at London they are

now about 700,000. Moreover the ground within the walls of old Rome was a circle but of three miles diameter, whose area is about seven square miles, and the suburbs scarce as much more, in all about thirteen square miles, whereas the built ground at London is about nine square miles as aforesaid; which two sorts of proportions agree with each other, and consequently old Rome seems but to have been half as big again as the present London, which we offer to antiquaries.

THE THIRD ESSAY.

Proofs that the number of people in the 134 parishes of the London bills of mortality, without reference to other cities, is about 696,000, viz. -

I know but three ways of finding the same.

1. By the houses, and families, and heads living in each.

2. By the number of burials in healthful times, and by the proportion of those that live, to those that die.

3. By the number of those who die of the plague in pestilential years, in proportion to those that escape.

The First Way.

To know the number of houses, I used three methods, viz. -

1. The number of houses which were burnt A.D. 1666, which by authentic report was 13,200; next what proportion the people who died out of those houses, bore to the whole; which I find A.D. 1686, to be but one seventh part, but A.D. 1666 to be almost one-fifth, from whence I infer the whole housing of London A.D. 1666 to have been 66,000, then finding the burials A.D. 1666 to be to those of 1686 as 3 to 4,I pitch upon 88,000 to be the number of housing A.D. 1686.

2. Those who have been employed in making the general map of London, set forth in the year 1682, told me that in that year they had found above 84,000 houses to be in London, wherefore A.D. 1686, or in four years more, there might be one-tenth or 8,400 houses more (London doubling in forty years) so as the whole, A.D. 1686 might be 92,400.

3. I found that A.D. 1685, there were 29,325 hearths in Dublin, and 6,400 houses, and in London 388 thousand hearths, whereby there must have been at that rate 87,000 houses in London. Moreover I found that in Bristol there were in the same year 16,752 hearth; and 5,307 houses, and in London 388,000 hearths as aforesaid; at which rate there must have been 123,000 houses in London, and at a medium between Dublin and Bristol proportions 105,000 houses.

Lastly, by certificate from the hearth office, I find the houses within the bills of mortality to be 105,315.

Having thus found the houses, I proceed next to the number of families in them, and first I thought that if there were three or four families or kitchens in every house of Paris, there might be two families in one-tenth of the housing of London; unto which supposition, the common opinion of several friends doth concur with my own conjectures.

As to the number of heads in each family, I stick to Grant's observation in page --- of his fifth edition, that in tradesmen of London's families there be eight heads one with another, in families of higher ranks, above ten, and in the poorest near live, according to which proportions, I had upon another occasion pitched the medium of heads in all the families of England to be six and one-third, but quitting the fraction in this case, I agree with Monsieur Auzout for six.

To conclude, the houses of London being 105,315 and the addition of double families 10,531 more, in all 115,846; I multiplied the same by six, which produced 695,076 for the number of the people.

The Second Way.

I found that the years 1684 and 1685, being next each other, and both healthful, did wonderfully agree in their burials, viz., 1684 they were 23,202, and A.D. 1685 23,222, the medium whereof is 23,212; moreover that the christenings 1684 were 14,702, and those A.D. 1685 were 14,730, wherefore I multiplied the medium of burials 23,212 by 30, supposing that one dies out of 30 at London, which made the number of people 696,360 souls.

Now to prove that one dies out of 30 at London or thereabouts, I say -

1. That Grant in the --- page of his fifth edition, affirmeth from observation, that 3 died of 88 per annum which is near the same proportion.

2. I found that out of healthful places, and out of adult persons, there dies much fewer, as but one out of 50 among our parliament men, and that the kings of England having reigned 24 years one with another, probably lived above 30 years each.

3. Grant, page --- hath shown that but about one of 20 die per annum out of young children under 10 years old, and Monsieur Auzout thinks that but 1 of 40 die at Rome, out of the greater proportion of adult persons there, wherefore we still stick as a medium to the number 30.

4. In nine country parishes lying in several parts of England, I find that but one of 37 hath died per annum, or 311 out of 11,507, wherefore till I see another round number, grounded upon many observations, nearer than 30, I hope to have done pretty well in multiplying our burials by 30 to find the number of the people, the product being 696,360, and what we find by the families they are 695,076, as aforesaid.

The Third Way.

It was proved by Grant, that one-fifth of the people died of the plague, but A.D. 1665 there died of the plague near 98,000 persons, the quintuple whereof is 490,000 as the number of people in the year 1665, whereunto adding above one-third, as the increase between 1665 and 1686, the total is 653,000, agreeing well enough with the other two computations above mentioned.

Wherefore let the proportion of 1 to 30 continue till a better be put in its place.

Memorandum. That two or three hundred new houses would make a contiguity of two or three other great parishes, with the 134 already mentioned in the bills of mortality: and that an oval wall of about twenty miles in compass would enclose the same, and all the shipping at Deptford and Blackwall, and would also fence in 20,000 acres of land, and lay the foundation or designation of several vast advantages to the owners, and inhabitants of that ground, as also to the whole nation and government.

THE FOURTH ESSAY.

Concerning the proportions of People in the eight eminent Cities of Christendom undernamed, viz.:-

1. We have by the number of burials in healthful years, and by the proportion of the living to those who die yearly, as also by the number of houses and families within the 134 parishes called London, and the estimate of the heads in each, pitched upon the number of people in that city to be at a medium 695,718.

2. We have, by allowing that at Paris above 80,000 families, viz., 81,280, do live in 23,223 houses, 32 palaces, and 38 colleges, or that there are 81,280 kitchens within less than 24,000 street doors; as also by allowing 30 heads for every one that died necessarily there; we have pitched upon the number of people there at a medium to be 488,055, nor have we restrained them to 300,000, by allowing with Monsieur Auzout 6 heads for each of Moreri's

50,000 houses or families.

3. To Amsterdam we allow 187,350 souls, viz., 30 times the number of their burials, which were 6,245 in the year 1685.

4. To Venice we allow 134,000 souls, as found there in a special account taken by authority, about ten years since, when the city abounded with such as returned from Candia, then surrendered to the Turks.

5. To Rome we allow 119,000 Christians, and 6,000 Jews, in all 125,000 souls, according to an account sent thither of the same by Monsieur Auzout.

6. To Dublin we allow (as to Amsterdam) 30 times its burials, the medium whereof for the last two years is 2,303, viz., 69,090 souls.

7. As to Bristol, we say that if the 6,400 houses of Dublin give 69,090 people, that the 5,307 houses of Bristol must give above 56,000 people. Moreover, if the 29,325 hearths of Dublin give 69,090 people, the 16,752 hearths of Bristol must give about 40,000; but the medium of 56,000 and 40,000 is 48,000.

8. As for Rouen, we have no help, but Monsieur Auzout's fancy of 80,000 souls to be in that city, and the conjecture of knowing men that Rouen is between the one-seventh and one-eighth part of Paris, and also that it is by a third bigger than Bristol; by all which, we estimate, till farther light, that Rouen hath at most but 66,000 people in it.

Now it may be wondered why we mentioned Rouen at all, having had so little knowledge of it; whereunto we answer, that we did not think it just to compare London with Paris, as to shipping and foreign trade, without adding Rouen thereunto, Rouen being to Paris as that part of London which is below the bridge, is to what is above it.

All which we heartily submit to the correction of the curious and candid, in the meantime observing according to the gross numbers under-mentioned.

London 696,000 Paris 488,000 Amsterdam 187,000 Venice 134,000 Rome 125,000 Dublin 69,000 Bristol 48,000 Rouen 66,000

Observations on the said Eight Cities.

1. That the people of Paris being 488,000 Rome 125,000 Rouen 66,000 do make in all but 679,000

or 17,000 less than the 696,000 of London alone.

2. That the people of the two English cities and emporiums--viz., of London, 696,000, and Bristol, 48,000--do make 744,000, or more than

In Paris 488,000 Amsterdam 187,090 Rouen 66,000 Being in all 741,000

3. That the same two English cities seem equivalent

To Paris, which hath 488,000 souls. Rouen 66,000 Lyons 100,000 Toulouse 90,000 In all 744,000

If there be any error in these conjectures concerning these cities of France, we hope they will be mended by those whom we hear to be now at work upon that matter.

4. That the King of England's three cities, viz.

London 696,000 { Paris 488,000 Dublin 69,000 exceed { Amsterdam 187,000 Bristol 48,000 { Venice 134,000 In all 813,000 Being but 809,000

5. That of the four great emporiums, London, Amsterdam, Venice, and Rouen, London alone is near double to the other three, viz., above 7 to 4.

Amsterdam 187,000 } Venice 134,000 } 387,000 Rouen 66,000 } 2 774,000

London 696,000

6. That London, for aught appears, is the greatest and most considerable city of the world, but manifestly the greatest emporium.

When these assertions have passed the examen of the critics, we shall make another essay, showing how to apply those truths to the honour and profit of the King and Kingdom of England.

THE FIFTH ESSAY.

Concerning Holland and the rest of the United Provinces.

Since the close of this paper, it hath been objected from Holland, that what hath been said of the number of houses and people in London is not like to be true; for that if it were, then London would be the two-thirds of the whole Province of Holland. To which is answered, that London is the two-thirds of all Holland, and more, that province having not 1,044,000 inhabitants (whereof 696,000 is the two-thirds), nor above 800,000, as we have credibly and often heard. For suppose Amsterdam hath--as we have elsewhere noted--187,000, the seven next great cities at 30,000 each, one with another, 210,000, the ten next at 15,000 each 150,000, the ten smallest at 6,000 each 60,000--in all, the twenty-eight walled cities and towns of Holland 607,000; in the dorps and villages 193,000, which is about one head for every four acres of land; whereas in England there is eight acres for every head, without the cities and market-towns.

Now, suppose London, having 116,000 families, should have seven heads in each--the medium between MM. Auzout's and Grant's reckonings--the total of the people would be 812,000; or if we reckon that there dies one out of thirty-four--the medium between thirty and thirty-seven above mentioned--the total of the people would be thirty-four times 23,212, viz., 789,208, the medium between which number and the above 812,000 is 800,604, somewhat exceeding 800,000, the supposed number of Holland.

Furthermore, I say that upon former searches into the peopling of the world, I never found that in any country--not in China itself-- there was more than one man to every English acre of land: many territories passing for well-peopled where there is but one man for ten such acres. I found by measuring Holland and West Frisia (alias North Holland) upon the best maps, that it contained but as many such acres as London doth of people, viz., about 696,000 acres. I therefore venture to pronounce (till better informed) that the people of London are as many as those of Holland, or at least above two-thirds of the same, which is enough to disable the objection above mentioned; nor is there any need to strain up London from 696,000 to 800,000, though competent reasons have been given to that purpose, and though the author of the excellent map of London, set forth A.D. 1682, reckoned the people thereof (as by the said map appears) to be 1,200,000, even when he thought the houses of the same to be but 85,000.

The worthy person who makes this objection in the same letter also saith -

1. That the province of Holland hath as many people as the other six united provinces together, and as the whole kingdom of England, and double to the city of Paris and its suburbs; that is to say, 2,000,000 souls. 2. He says that in London and Amsterdam, and other trading cities, there are ten heads to every family, and that in Amsterdam there are not 22,000 families. 3. He excepteth against the register alleged by Monsieur Auzout, which makes 23,223 houses and above 80,000 families to be in Paris; as also against the register alleged by Petty, making 105,315 houses to be in London, with a tenth part of the same to be of families more than houses; and probably will except against the register of 1,163 houses to be in all England, that number giving, at six and one-third heads to each family, about 7,000,000 people, upon all which we remark as follows, viz.:-

1. That if Paris doth contain but 488,000 souls, that then all Holland containeth but the double of that number, or 976,000, wherefore London, containing 696,000 souls, hath above two-thirds of all Holland by 46,000.

2. If Paris containeth half as many people as there are in all England, it must contain 3,500,000 souls, or above seven times 488,000; and because there do not die 20,000 per annum out of Paris, there must die but one out of 175; whereas Monsieur Auzout thinks that there dies one out of 25, and there must live 149 heads in every house of Paris mentioned in the register, but there must be scarce two heads in every house of England, all which we think fit to be reconsidered.

I must, as an Englishman, take notice of one point more, which is, that these assertions do reflect upon the empire of England, for that it is said that England hath but 2,000,000 inhabitants, and it might as well have been added, that Scotland and Ireland, with the Islands of Man, Jersey, and Guernsey, have but two-fifths of the same number, or 800,000 more, or that all the King of England's subjects in Europe are but 2,800,000 souls, whereas he saith that the subjects of the seven united provinces are 4,000,000. To which we answer that the subjects of the said seven provinces are, by this objector's own showing, but the quadruple of Paris, or 1,932,000 souls, Paris containing but 488,000, as afore hath been proved, and we do here affirm that England hath 7,000,000 people, and that Scotland, Ireland, with the Islands of Man, Jersey, and Guernsey, hath two-fifths of the said number, or 2,800,000 more, in all 9,800,000; whereas by the objector's doctrine, if the seven provinces have 1,932,000 people, the King of England's territories should have but seven-tenths of the same number, viz., 1,351,000, whereas we say 9,800,000, as aforesaid, which difference is so gross as that it deserves to be thus reflected upon.

To conclude, we expect from the concerned critics of the world that they would prove -

1. That Holland, and West Frisia, and the twenty-eight towns and cities thereof, hath more people than London alone.

2. That any three of the best cities of France, any two of all Christendom, or

any one of the world, hath the same, or better housing, and more foreign trade than London, even in the year that King James the Second came to the empire thereof.

OF THE PEOPLE OF ENGLAND.

Founded upon the Calculations of Gregory King, Lancaster Herald, and forming part of "An Essay upon the Probable Methods of making a People gainers in the Balance of Trade." Published in 1699.

The writer of these papers has seen the natural and political observations and conclusions upon the state and condition of England by Gregory King, Esq., Lancaster Herald, in manuscript. The calculations therein contained are very accurate, and more perhaps to be relied upon than anything that has been ever done of the like kind. This skilful and laborious gentleman has taken the right course to form his several schemes about the numbers of the people, for besides many different ways of working, he has very carefully inspected the poll-books, and the distinctions made by those acts, and the produce in many of the respective polls, going everywhere by reasonable and discreet mediums: besides which pains, he has made observations of the very facts in particular towns and places, from which he has been able to judge and conclude more safely of others, so that he seems to have looked further into this mystery than any other person.

With his permission, we shall offer to the public such of his computations as may be of use, and enlighten in the matter before us.

He lays down that if the first peopling of England was by a colony or colonies, consisting of a number between 100 and 1,000 people (which seems probable), such colony or colonies might be brought over between the year of the world 2400 and 2600, viz., about 800 or 900 years after the Flood, and 1,400 or 1,500 years before the birth of Christ, at which time the world might have about 1,000,000 families, and 4,000,000 or 5,000,000 people.

From which hypothesis it will follow by an orderly series of increase -

That when the Romans invaded England fifty-three years before Christ's time, the kingdom might have about 360,000 people, and at Christ's birth about 400,000.

That at the Norman Conquest, A.D. 1066, the kingdom might contain somewhat above 2,000,000.

That A.D. 1260, or about 200 years after the Norman Conquest, it might contain about 2,750,000 people, or half the present number: so that the people of England may have doubled in about 435 years last past.

That in all probability the next doubling will be in about 600 years to come, viz., by the year 2300, at which time it may have about 11,000,000 people, and the kingdom containing about 39,000,000 of acres, there will be then about three acres and a half per head.

That the increase of the kingdom for every hundred years of the last preceding term of doubling, and the subsequent term of doubling, may have been and in all probability may be, according to the following scheme:-

Anno Number of Increase every Domini. people. hundred years. 1300 2,800,000 1400 3,300,000 440,000. 1500 3,840,000 540,000. 1600 4,620,000 780,000. 1700 5,500,000 880,000. 1800 6,420,000 920,000. 1900 7,350,000 930,000. 2000 8,280,000 930,000. 2100 9,205,000 925,000. 2200 10,115,000 910,000. 2300 11,000,000 885,000.

Whereby it may appear that the increase of the kingdom being 880,000 people in the last hundred years, and 920,000 in the next succeeding hundred years, the annual increase at this time may be about 9,000 souls per annum.

But whereas the yearly births of the kingdom are about 1 in 28.95, or 190,000 souls. And the yearly burials 1 in 32.35 or 170,000 souls. Whereby the yearly increase would be 20,000 souls.

It is to be noted-- Per ann.

1. That the allowance for plagues and great mortalities may come to at a medium 4,000 2. Foreign or civil wars at a medium 3,500 3. The sea constantly employing 11,000 per annum. about 40,000, may precipitate 2,500 the death of about 4. The plantations (over and above the accession of foreigners) 1,000 may carry away Whereby the net annual increase may be but 9,000 souls.

That of these 20,000 souls, which would be the annual increase of the kingdom by procreation, were it not for the before-mentioned abatements.

The country increases annually by procreation 20,000 souls. The cities and towns, exclusive of London, by procreation 2,000 souls. But London and the bills of mortality decrease annually 2,000 souls.

So that London requires a supply of 2,000 souls per annum to keep it from decreasing, besides a further supply of about 3,000 per annum for its increase at this time. In all 5,000, or above a half of the kingdom's net increase.

Mr. King further observes that by the assessments on marriages, births, and burials, and the collectors' returns thereupon, and by the parish registers, it appears that the proportions of marriages, births, and burials are according to the following scheme

Vide Scheme A.

Whence it may be observed that in 10,000 coexisting persons there are 71 or 72 marriages in the country, producing 343 children; 78 marriages in towns producing 351 children; 94 marriages in London, producing 376 children.

Whereby it follows -

1. That though each marriage in London produces fewer people than in the country, yet London in general having a greater proportion of breeders, is more prolific than the other great towns, and the great towns are more prolific than the country.

2. That if the people of London of all ages were as long-lived as those in the country, London would increase in people much faster pro rata than the country.

3. That the reasons why each marriage in London produces fewer children than the country marriages seem to be -

(1) From the more frequent fornications and adulteries.

(2) From a greater luxury and intemperance.

(3) From a greater intentness on business.

(4) From the unhealthfulness of the coal smoke.

(5) From a greater inequality of age between the husbands and wives.

(6) From the husbands and wives not living so long as in the country.

He further observes, accounting the people to be 5,500,000, that the said five millions and a half (including the transitory people and vagrants) appear by the assessments on marriages, births, and burials, to bear the following proportions in relation to males and females, and other distinctions of the people, viz.:-

SCHEMA A

People Annual Marriages Producing

children In all each

530,000 London and bills of mortality 1 in 106 5,000 4.0 870,000 The cities and market towns 1 in 128 6,800 4.5 4,100,000 The villages and hamlets 1 in 141 29,200 4.8 5,500,000 1 in 134 41,000 4.64

Annual Births Annual Burials In all In all London and bills of mortality 1 in 26.5 20,000 1 in 24.1 22,000 The cities and market towns 1 in 28.5 30,600 1 in 30.4 28,600 The villages and hamlets 1 in 29.4 29,200 1 in 34.4 119,400 1 in 28.95 190,000 1 in 32.35 170,000

Vide Scheme B.

So that the number of communicants is in all 3,260,000 souls; and the number of fighting men between sixteen and sixty is 1,308,000.

SCHEME B.

Males Females Males Females Both In London and 10 to 13 230,000 300,000 530,000 bills of mortality In the other cities 8 to 9 410,000 460,000 870,000 and market-towns In the villages and 100 to 99 2,060,000 2,040,000 4,100,000 hamlets 27 to 28 2,700,000 2,800,000 5,500,000

That as to other distinctions they appear by the said assessments to bear these proportions.

People. Males. Females. Husbands and wives 1,900,000 950,000 950,000 at above, 34.5% Widowers at above 1.5% 90,000 90,000 Widows at about 4.5% 240,000 240,000 Children at above 45% 2,500,000 1,300,000 1,200,000 Servants at about 10.5% 560,000 260,000 300,000 Sojourners and single persons 4% 210,000 100,000 110,000 100% 5,500,000 2,700,000 2,800,000

And that the different proportions in each of the said articles between London, the great towns, and the villages, may the better appear, he has formed the following scheme:-

London and Bills The other Cities The Villages and of Mortality. and great Towns. Hamlets. Souls. Souls. Souls. Husbands and Wives 37% 196,100 36% 313,200 34% 1,394,000 Widowers 2% 10,600 2% 17,400 1.5% 61,500 Widows 7% 37,100 6% 52,200 4.5% 184,500 Children 33% 174,900 40% 348,000 47% 1,927,000 Servants 13% 68,900 11% 95,700 10% 410,000 Sojourners 8% 42,400 5% 43,500 3% 123,000 100% 530,000 100% 870,000 100% 4,100,000

SCHEME B (Continued)

He further observes, supposing the people to be 5,500,000, that the yearly births of the Kingdom may be 190,000, and that the several ages of the people may be as follows:

In all Males Females Those under 1 years old 170,000 88,500 81,500 Those under 5 years old 820,000 413,300 406,700 Those under 10 years old 1,520,000 762,900 757,100 Those above 16 years old 3,260,000 1,578,000 1,682,000 Those above 21 years old 2,700,000 1,300,000 1,400,000 Those above 25 years old 2,400,000 1,152,000 1,248,000 Those above 60 years old 600,000 270,000 330,000 Those under 16 years old 2,240,000 Those above 16 years old 3,260,000 Total of the people 5,500,000

That the bachelors are about 28 per cent. of the whole, whereof those under twenty-five years are 25.5 per cent., and those above twenty-five years are 2.5 per cent.

That the maidens are about 28.5 per cent. of the whole.

Whereof those under 25 years are 26.5 per cent.

And those above 25 years are 2 per cent.

That the males and females in the kingdom in general are aged, one with another, 27 years and a half.

That in the kingdom in general there is near as many people living under 20 years of age as there is above 20, whereof half of the males are under 19, and one half of the females are under 21 years.

That the ages of the people, according to their several distinctions, are as follows, viz.:-

Vide Scheme C.

Having thus stated the numbers of the people, he gives a scheme of the income and expense of the several families of England, calculated for the year 1688.

SCHEME C

The husbands are aged 43 years apiece, which, at 17.25% makes 742 years. The wives 40 17.25% 690 The widowers 56 1.5% 84 The widows 60 4.5% 270 The children 12 45% 540 The servants 27 10.5% 284 The sojourners 35 4% 140 At a medium 27.5 100 2,750

Vide Scheme D.

Mr. King's modesty has been so far overruled as to suffer us to communicate these his excellent computations, which we can the more safely commend, having examined them very carefully, tried them by some little operations of our own upon the same subject, and compared them with the schemes of other persons, who take pleasure in the like studies.

What he says concerning the number of the people to be 5,500,000 is no positive assertion, nor shall we pretend anywhere to determine in that matter;

what he lays down is by way of hypothesis, that supposing the inhabitants of England to have been, A.D. 1300, 2,860,000 heads, by the orderly series of increase allowed of by all writers they may probably be about A.D. 1700, 5,500,000 heads; but if they were A.D. 1300 either less or more, the case must proportionably alter; for as to his allowances for plagues, great mortalities, civil wars, the sea, and the plantations, they seem very reasonable, and not well to be controverted.

Upon these schemes of Mr. King we shall make several remarks, though the text deserves much a better comment.

SCHEME D.--A SCHEME OF THE INCOME AND EXPENSE OF THE SEVERAL FAMILIES OF ENGLAND, CALCULATED FOR THE YEAR 1688 Number of Ranks, Degrees and Heads per Families. Qualifications Family. 160 Temporal Lords 40 26 Spiritual Lords 20 800 Baronets 16 600 Knights 13 3,000 Esquires 10 12,000 Gentlemen 8 5,000 Persons in greater offices and places 8 5,000 Persons in lesser offices and places 6 2,000 Eminent merchants and traders by sea 8 8,000 Lesser merchants and traders by sea 6 10,000 Persons in the law 7 2,000 Eminent clergymen 6 8,000 Lesser clergymen 5 40,000 Freeholders of the better sort 7 120,000 Freeholders of the lesser sort 5.5 150,000 Farmers 5 15,000 Persons in liberal arts and sciences 5 50,000 Shopkeepers and tradesmen 4.5 60,000 Artisans and handicrafts 4 5,000 Naval officers 4 4,000 Military officers 4 500,586 5.33 50,000 Common seamen 3 364,000 Labouring people and out-servants 3.5 400,000 Cottagers and paupers 3.25 35,000 Common soldiers 2 849,000 Vagrants, as gipsies, thieves, beggars, &c. 3.25 500,586 Increasing the wealth of the kingdom 5.33 849,000 Decreasing the wealth of the kingdom 3.25 1,349,586 Net totals 4 1/13

[The previous table continues but is too wide for the page. It has been split down the middle--DP.]

Number Yearly Yearly Yearly Yearly Yearly Yearly of Income Income Income Expense Increase Incr. Persons per. in per. per per. in Family general

Hd. Hd. Hd. General P. s. P. P. s. P. s. d. P.s. d. P. 6,400 3,200 0 512,000 80 0 70 0 0 10 0 0 64,000 520 1,300 0 33,800 65 0 45 0 0 20 0 0 10,400 12,800 880 0 704,000 55 0 49 0 0 6 0 0 76,800 7,800 650 0 390,000 50 0 45 0 0 5 0 0 39,000 30,000 450 0 1,200,000 45 0 41 0 0 4 0 0 120,000 96,000 280 0 2,880,000 35 0 32 0 0 3 0 0 288,000 40,000 240 0 1,200,000 30 0 26 0 0 4 0 0 160,000 30,000 120 0 600,000 20 0 17 0 0 3 0 0 90,000 16,000 400 0 800,000 50 0 37 0 0 13 0 0 208,000 48,000 198 0 1,600,000 33 0 27 0 0 6 0 0 288,000 70,000 154 0 1,540,000 22 0 18 0 0 4 0 0 280,000 12,000 72 0 144,000 12 0 10 0 0 2 0 0 24,000 40,000 50 0 400,000 10 0 9 4 0 0 16 0 32,000 280,000 91 0 3,640,000 13 0 11 15 0 1 5 0 350,000 660,000 55 0 6,600,000 10 0 9 10 0 0 10 0 330,000 750,000 42 10 6,375,000 8 10 8 5 0 0 5 0 187,500 75,000 60 0 900,000 12 0 11 0 0 1 0 0 75,000 225,000 45 0 2,250,000 10 0 9 0 0 1 0 0 225,000 240,000 38 0 2,280,000 9 10 9 0 0 0 10 0 120,000 20,000 80 0 400,000 20 0 18 0 0 2 0 0 40,000 16,000 60 0 240,000 15 0 14 0 0 1 0 0 16,000 2,675,520 68 18 34,488,800 12 18 ll 15 4 1 2 8 3,023,700 Decrease.Decrease. 150,000 20 0 1,000,000 7 0 7 10 0 0 10 0 75,000 1,275,000 15 0 5,460,000 4 10 4 12 0 0 2 0 127,500 1,300,000 6 10 2,000,000 2 0 2 5 0 0 5 0 325,000 70,000 14 0 490,000 7 0 7 10 0 0 10 0 35,000 2,795,000 10 10 8,950,000 3 5 3 9 0 0 4 0 562,500 30,000 60,000 2 0 4 0 0 2 0 0 60,000 So the General Account is 2,675,520 68 18 34,488,800 12 18 11 15 4 1 2 8 3,023,700 2,825,000 10 10 9,010,000 3 3 3 7 6 0 4 6 622,500 5,500,520 32 5 43,491,800 7 18 7 9 3 0 8 9 2,401,200

The people being the first matter of power and wealth, by whose labour and industry a nation must be gainers in the balance, their increase or decrease must be carefully observed by any government that designs to thrive; that is, their increase must be promoted by good conduct and wholesome laws, and if they have been decreased by war, or any other accident, the breach is to be made up as soon as possible, for it is a maim in the body politic affecting all its parts.

Almost all countries in the world have been more or less populous, as liberty and property have been there well or ill secured. The first constitution of Rome was no ill-founded government, a kingly power limited by laws; and the people increased so fast, that, from a small beginning, in the reign of their sixth king were they able to send out an army of 80,000 men. And in the time of the commonwealth, in that invasion which the Gauls made upon Italy, not long before Hannibal came thither, they were grown so numerous, as that their troops consisted of 700,000 foot and 70,000 horse; it is true their allies were comprehended in this number, but the ordinary people fit to bear arms being mustered in Rome and Campania, amounted to 250,000 foot and 23,000 horse.

Nothing, therefore, can more contribute to the rendering England populous and strong than to have liberty upon a right footing, and our legal constitution firmly preserved. A nation may be as well called free under a limited kingship as in a commonwealth, and it is to this good form of our government that we partly owe that doubling of the people which has probably happened here in the 435 years last past. And if the ambition of some, and the mercenary temper of others, should bring us at any time to alter our constitution, and to give up our ancient rights, we shall find our numbers diminish visibly and fast. For liberty encourages procreation, and not only keeps our own inhabitants among us, but invites strangers to come and live under the shelter of our laws.

The Romans, indeed, made use of an adventitious help to enlarge their city, which was by incorporating foreign cities and nations into their commonwealth; but this way is not without its mischiefs. For the strangers in Rome by degrees had grown so numerous, and to have so great a vote in the councils, that the whole Government began to totter, and decline from its old to its new inhabitants, which Fabius the censor observing, he applied a remedy in time by reducing all the new citizens into four tribes, that being contracted into so narrow a space, they might not have so malignant an influence upon the city.

An Act of general naturalisation would likewise probably increase our numbers very fast, and repair what loss we may have suffered in our people by the late war. It is a matter that has been very warmly contended for by many good patriots; but peradventure it carries also its danger with it, which perhaps would have the less influence by this expedient, namely, if an Act of

Parliament were made, that no heads of families hereafter to be naturalised for the first generation, should have votes in any of our elections. But as the case stands, it seems against the nature of right government that strangers (who may be spies, and who may have an interest opposite to that of England, and who at best ever join in one link of obsequiousness to the Ministers) should be suffered to intermeddle in that important business of sending members to Parliament. From their sons indeed there is less to fear, who by birth and nature may come to have the same interest and inclinations as the natives.

And though the expedient of Fabius Maximus, to contract the strangers into four tribes, might be reasonable where the affairs of a whole empire were transacted by magistrates chosen in one city, yet the same policy may not hold good in England; foreigners cannot influence elections here by being dispersed about in the several counties of the kingdom, where they can never come to have any considerable strength. But some time or other they may endanger the government by being suffered to remain, such vast numbers of them here in London where they inhabit altogether, at least 30,000 persons in two quarters of the town, without intermarrying with the English, or learning our language, by which means for several years to come they are in a way still to continue foreigners, and perhaps may have a foreign interest and foreign inclinations; to permit this cannot be advisable or safe. It may therefore be proper to limit any new Acts of naturalisation with such restrictions as may make the accession of strangers not dangerous to the public.

An accession of strangers, well regulated, may add to our strength and numbers; but then it must be composed of labouring men, artificers, merchants, and other rich men, and not of foreign soldiers, since such fright and drive away from a nation more people than their troops can well consist of: for if it has been ever seen that men abound most where there is most freedom (China excepted, whose climate excels all others, and where the exercise of the tyranny is mild and easy) it must follow that people will in time desert those countries whose best flower is their liberties, if those liberties are thought precarious or in danger. That foreign soldiers are dangerous to liberty, we may produce examples from all countries and all ages; but we shall instance only one, because it is eminent above all the rest.

The Carthaginians, in their wars, did very much use mercenary and foreign troops; and when the peace was made between them and the Romans, after a long dispute for the dominion of Sicily, they brought their army home to be paid and disbanded, which Gesco, their General, had the charge of embarking, who did order all his part with great dexterity and wisdom. But the State of Carthage wanting money to clear arrears, and satisfy the troops, was forced to keep them up longer than was designed. The army consisted of Gauls, Ligurians, Baleareans, and Greeks. At first they were insolent in their quarters in Carthage, and were prevailed upon to remove to Sicca, where they were to remain and expect their pay. There they grew presently corrupted with ease and pleasure, and fell into mutinies and disorder, and to making extravagant demands of pay and gratuities; and in a rage, with their arms in their hands, they marched 20,000 of them towards Carthage, encamping within fifteen miles of the city; and chose Spendius and Matho, two profligate wretches, for their leaders, and imprisoned Gesco, who was deputed to them from the commonwealth. Afterwards they caused almost all the Africans, their tributaries, to revolt; they grew in a short time to be 70,000 strong; they fought several battles with Hanno and Hamilcar Barcas. During these transactions, the mercenaries that were in garrison in Sardinia mutinied likewise, murdering their commander and all the Carthaginians; while Spendius and Matho, to render their accomplices more desperate, put Gesco to a cruel death, presuming afterwards to lay siege to Carthage itself. They met with a shock indeed at Prion, where 40,000 of them were slaughtered; but soon after this battle, in another they took one of the Carthaginian generals prisoner, whom they fixed to a cross, crucifying thirty of the principal senators round about him. Spendius and Matho were at last taken, the one crucified and the other tormented to death: but the war lasted three years and near four months with excessive cruelty; in which the State of Carthage lost several battles, and was often brought within a hair's-breadth of utter ruin.

If so great a commonwealth as Carthage, though assisted at that time by Hiero, King of Syracuse, and by the Romans, ran the hazard of losing their empire, city, and liberties, by the insurrection of a handful of mercenaries, whose first strength was but 20,000 men; it should be a warning to all free nations how they suffer armies so composed to be among them, and it should frighten a wise State from desiring such an increase of people as may be had by the bringing over foreign soldiers.

Indeed, all armies whatsoever, if they are over-large, tend to the dispeopling of a country, of which our neighbour nation is a sufficient proof, where in one of the best climates in Europe men are wanting to till the ground. For children do not proceed from the intemperate pleasures taken loosely and at random, but from a regular way of living, where the father of the family desires to rear up and provide for the offspring he shall beget.

Securing the liberties of a nation may be laid down as a fundamental for increasing the numbers of its people; but there are other polities thereunto conducing which no wise State has ever neglected.

No race of men did multiply so fast as the Jews, which may be attributed chiefly to the wisdom of Moses their Lawgiver, in contriving to promote the state of marriage.

The Romans had the same care, paying no respect to a man childless by his own fault, and giving great immunities and privileges, both in the city and provinces, to those who had such and such a number of children. Encouragements of the like kind are also given in France to such as enrich the commonwealth by a large issue.

But we in England have taken another course, laying a fine upon the marriage bed, which seems small to those who only contemplate the pomp and wealth round about them, and in their view; but they who look into all the different ranks of men are well satisfied that this duty on marriages and births is a very grievous burden upon the poorer sort, whose numbers compose the strength and wealth of any nation. This tax was introduced by the necessity of affairs. It is difficult to say what may be the event of a new thing; but if we are to take measures from past wisdom, which exempted prolific families from public duties, we should not lay impositions upon those who find it hard enough to maintain themselves. If this tax be such a weight upon the poor as to discourage marriage and hinder propagation, which seems the truth, no doubt it ought to be abolished; and at a convenient time we ought to change it for some other duty, if there were only this single reason, that it is so directly opposite to the polity of all ages and all countries.

In order to have hands to carry on labour and manufactures, which must make us gainers in the balance of trade, we ought not to deter, but rather invite men to marry, which is to be done by privileges and exemptions for such a number of children, and by denying certain offices of trust and dignities to all unmarried persons; and where it is once made a fashion among those of the better sort, it will quickly obtain with the lower degree.

Mr. King, in his scheme (for which he has as authentic grounds as perhaps the matter is capable of) lays down that the annual marriages of England are about 41,000, which is one marriage out of every 134 persons. Upon which, we observe, that this is not a due proportion, considering how few of our adult males (in comparison with other countries) perish by war or any other accident; from whence may be inferred that our polity is some way or other defective, or the marriages would bear a nearer proportion with the gross number of our people; for which defect, if a remedy can be found, there will be so much more strength added to the kingdom.

From the books of assessment on births, marriages, &c., by the nearest view he can make, he divides the 5,500,000 people into 2,700,000 males and 2,800,000 females; from whence (considering the females exceed the males in number, and considering that the men marry later than women, and that many of the males are of necessity absent in the wars, at sea, and upon other business) it follows that a large proportion of the females remain unmarried, though at an adult age, which is a dead loss to the nation, every birth being as so much certain treasure, upon which account such laws must be for the public good, as induce all men to marry whose circumstances permit it.

From his division of the people it may be likewise observed, that the near proportion there is between the males and females (which is said to hold also in other places) is an argument (and the strongest that can be produced) against polygamy, and the increase of mankind which some think might be from thence expected; for if Nature had intended to one man a plurality of wives, she would have ordered a great many more female births than male, her designments being always right and wise.

The securing the parish for bastard children is become so small a punishment and so easily compounded, that it very much hinders marriage. The Dutch compel men of all ranks to marry the woman whom they have got with child, and perhaps it would tend to the further peopling of England if the common people here, under such a certain degree, were condemned by some new law to suffer the same penalty.

A country that makes provision to increase in inhabitants, whose situation is good, and whose people have a genius adapted to trade, will never fail to be gainers in the balance, provided the labour and industry of their people be well managed and carefully directed.

The more any man contemplates these matters the more he will come to be of opinion, that England is capable of being rendered one of the strongest nations, and the richest spot of ground in Europe.

It is not extent of territory that makes a country powerful, but numbers of men well employed, convenient ports, a good navy, and a soil producing all sort of commodities. The materials for all this we have, and so improvable, that if we did but second the gifts of Nature with our own industry we should soon arrive to a pitch of greatness that would put us at least upon an equal footing with any of our neighbours.

If we had the complement of men our land can maintain and nourish; if we had as much trade as our stock and knowledge in sea affairs is capable of embracing; if we had such a naval strength as a trade so extended would easily produce; and, if we had those stores and that wealth which is the certain result of a large and well-governed traffic, what human strength could hurt or invade us? On the contrary, should we not be in a posture not only to resist but to give the law to others?

Our neighbouring commonwealth has not in territory above 8,000,000 acres, and perhaps not much above 2,200,000 people, and yet what a figure have they made in Europe for these last 100 years? What wars have they maintained? What forces have they resisted? and to what a height of power are they now come, and all by good order and wise government?

They are liable to frequent invasions; they labour under the inconvenience and danger of bad ports; they consume immense sums every year to defend their land against the sea; all which difficulties they have subdued by an unwearied industry.

We are fenced by nature against foreign enemies, our ports are safe, we fear no irruptions of the sea, our land territory at home is at least 39,000,000 acres. We have in all likelihood not less than 5,500,000 people. What a nation might we then become, if all these advantages were thoroughly improved, and if a right application were made of all this strength and of these numbers?

They who apprehend the immoderate growth of any prince or State may, perhaps, succeed by beginning first, and by attempting to pull down such a dangerous neighbour, but very often their good designs are disappointed. In all appearance they proceed more safely, who, under such a fear, make themselves strong and powerful at home. And this was the course which Philip, King of Macedon, the father of Perseus, took, when he thought to be invaded by the Romans.

The greatness of Rome gave Carthage very anxious thoughts, and it rather seems that they entered into the second Punic War more for fear the Romans should have the universal empire, than out of any ambition to lord it themselves over the whole world. Their design was virtuous, and peradventure wise to endeavour at some early interruption to a rival that grew so fast. However, we see they miscarried, though their armies were led by Hannibal. But fortune which had determined the dominion of the earth for Rome, did, perhaps, lead them into the fatal counsel of passing the Eber contrary to the articles of peace concluded with Asdrubal, and of attacking Saguntum before they had sufficiently recovered of the wounds they had suffered in the wars about Sicily, Sardinia, and with their own rebels. If the high courage of Hannibal had not driven the commonwealth into a new war while it was yet faint and weak, and if they had been suffered to pursue their victories in Spain, and to get firm footing in that rich, warlike, and then populous country, very probably in a few years they might have been a more equal match for the Roman people. It is true, if the Romans had endeavoured, at the conquest of Spain, and if they had disturbed the Carthaginians in that country, the war must have been unavoidable, because it was evident in that age, and will be apparent in the times we live in, that whatever foreign power, already grown great, can add to its dominion the possession of Spain, will stand fair for universal empire.

But unless some such cogent reason of state, as is here instanced, intervene, in all appearance the best way for a nation that apprehends the growing power of any neighbour is to fortify itself within; we do not mean by land armies, which rather debilitate than strengthen a country, but by potent navies, by thrift in the public treasure, care of the people's trade, and all the other honest and useful arts of peace.

By such an improvement of our native strength, agreeable to the laws and to the temper of a free nation, England without doubt may be brought to so good a posture and condition of defending itself, as not to apprehend any neighbour jealous of its strength or envious of its greatness.

And to this end we open these schemes, that a wise Government under which we live, not having any designs to become arbitrary, may see what materials they have to work upon, and how far our native wealth is able to second their good intentions of preserving us a rich and a free people.

Having said something of the number of our inhabitants, we shall proceed to discourse of their different degrees and ranks, and to examine who are a burden and who are a profit to the public, for by how much every part and member of the commonwealth can be made useful to the whole, by so much a nation will be more and more a gainer in this balance of trade which we are to treat of.

Mr. King, from the assessments on births and marriages, and from the polls, has formed the scheme here inserted, of the ranks, degrees, titles and qualifications of the people. He has done it so judiciously, and upon such grounds, that is well worth the careful perusal of any curious person, from thence we shall make some observations in order to put our present matter in a clearer light.

First, this scheme detects their error, who in the calculation they frame contemplate nothing but the wealth and plenty they see in rich cities and great towns, and from thence make a judgment of the kingdom's remaining part, and from this view conclude that taxes and payments to the public do mostly arise from the gentry and better sort, by which measures they neither contrive their imposition aright, nor are they able to give a true estimate what it shall produce; but when we have divided the inhabitants of England into their proper classes, it will appear that the nobility and gentry are but a small part of the whole body of the people.

Believing that taxes fell chiefly upon the better sort, they care not what they lay, as thinking they will not be felt; but when they come to be levied, they either fall short, and so run the public into an immense debt, or they light so heavily upon the poorer sort, as to occasion insufferable clamours; and they, whose proper business it was to contrive these matters better have been so unskilful, that the legislative power has been more than once compelled for the peoples' ease to give new funds, instead of others that had been ill projected.

This may be generally said, that all duties whatsoever upon the consumption of a large produce, fall with the greatest weight upon the common sort, so that such as think in new duties that they chiefly tax the rich will find themselves quite mistaken; for either their fund must yield little, or it must arise from the whole body of the people, of which the richer sort are but a small proportion.

And though war, and national debts and engagements, might heretofore very rationally plead for excises upon our home consumption, yet now there is a peace, it is the concern of every man that loves his country to proceed warily in laying new ones, and to get off those which are already laid as fast as ever he can. High customs and high excises both together are incompatible, either of them alone are to be endured, but to have them co-exist is suffered in no well- governed nation. If materials of foreign growth were at an easy rate, a high price might be the better borne in things of our own product, but to have both dear at once (and by reason of the duties laid upon them) is ruinous to the inferior rank of men, and this ought to weigh more with us, when we consider that even of the common people a subdivision is to be made, of which one part subsist from their own havings, arts, labour, and industry; and the other part subsist a little from their own labour, but chiefly from the help and charity of the rank that is above them. For according to Mr. King's scheme -

The nobility and gentry, with their families and retainers, the persons in offices, merchants, persons in the law, the clergy, freeholders, farmers, persons in sciences and liberal arts, shopkeepers, and tradesmen, handicrafts, men, naval officers, with the families and dependants upon all these altogether, make up the number of 2,675,520 heads.

The common seamen, common soldiers, labouring people, and out- servants, cottagers, paupers, and their families, with the vagrants, make up the number of 2,825,000 heads.

In all 5,500,520 heads.

So that here seems a majority of the people, whose chief dependence and subsistence is from the other part, which majority is much greater, in respect of the number of families, because 500,000 families contribute to the support of 850,000 families. In contemplation of which, great care should be taken not to lay new duties upon the home consumption, unless upon the extremest necessities of the State; for though such impositions cannot be said to fall directly upon the lower rank, whose poverty hinders them from consuming such materials (though there are few excises to which the meanest person does not pay something), yet indirectly, and by unavoidable consequences, they are rather more affected by high duties upon our home-consumption than the wealthier degree of people, and so we shall find the case to be, if we look carefully into all the distinct ranks of men there enumerated.

First, as to the nobility and gentry, they must of necessity retrench their families and expenses, if excessive impositions are laid upon all sorts of materials for consumption, from whence follows, that the degree below them of merchants, shopkeepers, tradesmen, and artisans, must want employment.

Secondly, as to the manufactures, high excises in time of peace are utterly destructive to that principal part of England's wealth; for if malt, coals, salt, leather, and other things, bear a great price, the wages of servants, workmen, and artificers, will consequently rise, for the income must bear some proportion with the expense; and if such as set the poor to work find wages for labour or manufacture advance upon them, they must rise in the price of their commodity, or they cannot live, all which would signify little, if nothing but our own dealings among one another were thereby affected; but it has a consequence far more pernicious in relation to our foreign trade, for it is the exportation of our own product that must make England rich; to be gainers in the balance of trade, we must carry out of our own product what will purchase the things of foreign growth that are needful for our own consumption, with some overplus either in bullion or goods to be sold in other countries, which overplus is the profit a nation makes by trade, and it is more or less according to the natural frugality of the people that export, or as from the low price of labour and manufacture they can afford the commodity cheap, and at a rate not to be undersold in foreign markets. The Dutch, whose labour and manufactures are dear by reason of home excises, can notwithstanding sell cheap abroad, because this disadvantage they labour under is balanced by the parsimonious temper of their people; but in England, where this frugality is hardly to be introduced, if the duties upon our home consumption are so large as to raise considerably the price of labour and manufacture, all our commodities for exportation must by degrees so advance in the prime value, that they cannot be sold at a rate which will give them vent in foreign markets, and we must be everywhere undersold by our wiser neighbours. But the consequence of such duties in times of peace will fall most heavily upon our woollen manufactures, of which most have more value from the workmanship than the material; and if the price of this workmanship be enhanced, it will in a short course of time put a necessity upon those we deal with of setting up manufactures of their own, such as they can, or of buying goods of the like kind and use from nations that can afford them cheaper. And in this point we are to consider, that the bulk of our woollen exports does not consist in draperies made of the fine wool, peculiar to our soil, but is composed of coarse broad cloths, such as Yorkshire cloths, kerseys, which make a great part of our exports, and may be, and are made of a coarser wool, which is to be had in other countries. So that we are not singly to value ourselves upon the material, but also upon the manufacture, which we should make as easy as we can, by not laying over-heavy burdens upon the manufacturer. And our woollen goods being two-thirds of our foreign exports, it ought to be the chief object of the public care, if we expect to be gainers in the balance of trade, which is what we hunt after in these inquiries.

Thirdly, as to the lower rank of all, which we compute at 2,825,000 heads, a majority of the whole people, their principal subsistence is upon the degrees above them, and if those are rendered uneasy these must share in the calamity, but even of this inferior sort no small proportion contribute largely to excises, as labourers and out-servants, which likewise affect the common seamen, who must thereupon raise their wages or they will not have wherewithal to keep their families left at home, and the high wages of seamen is another burden upon our foreign traffic. As to the cottagers, who are about a fifth part of the whole people, some duties reach even them, as those upon malt, leather, and salt, but not much because of their slender consumption, but if the gentry, upon whose woods and gleanings they live, and who employ them in day labour, and if the manufacturers, for whom they card and spin, are overburdened with duties, they cannot afford to give them so much for their labour and handiwork, nor to yield them those other reliefs which are their principal subsistence, for want of which these miserable wretches must perish with cold and hunger.

Thus we see excises either directly or indirectly fall upon the whole body of the people, but we do not take notice of these matters as receding from our former opinion. On the contrary, we still think them the most easy and equal way of taxing a nation, and perhaps it is demonstrable that if we had fallen into this method at the beginning of the war of raising the year's expense within the year by excises, England had not been now indebted so many millions, but what was advisable under such a necessity and danger is not to be pursued in times of peace, especially in a country depending so much upon trade and manufactures.

Our study now ought to be how those debts may be speedily cleared off, for which these new revenues are the funds, that trade may again move freely as it did heretofore, without such a heavy clog; but this point we shall more amply handle when we come to speak of our payments to the public.

Mr. King divides the whole body of the people into two principal classes, viz.:-

Increasing the wealth of the kingdom 2,675,520 heads. Decreasing the wealth of the kingdom 2,825,000 heads.

By which he means that the first class of the people from land, arts, and industry maintain themselves, and add every year something to the nation's general stock, and besides this, out of their superfluity, contribute every year so much to the maintenance of others.

That of the second class some partly maintain themselves by labour (as the heads of the cottage families), but that the rest, as most of the wives and children of these, sick and impotent people, idle beggars and vagrants, are nourished at the cost of others, and are a yearly burden to the public, consuming annually so much as would be otherwise added to the nation's general stock.

The bodies of men are, without doubt, the most valuable treasure of a country, and in their sphere the ordinary people are as serviceable to the commonwealth as the rich if they are employed in honest labour and useful arts, and such being more in number do more contribute to increase the nation's wealth than the higher rank.

But a country may be populous and yet poor (as were the ancient Gauls and Scythians), so that numbers, unless they are well employed, make the body politic big but unwieldy, strong but unactive, as to any uses of good government.

Theirs is a wrong opinion who think all mouths profit a country that consume its produce, and it may be more truly affirmed, that he who does not some way serve the commonwealth, either by being employed or by employing others, is not only a useless, but a hurtful member to it.

As it is charity, and what we indeed owe to human kind, to make provision for the aged, the lame, the sick, blind, and impotent, so it is a justice we owe to the commonwealth not to suffer such as have health, and who might maintain themselves, to be drones and live upon the labour of others.

The bulk of such as are a burden to the public consists in the cottagers and paupers, beggars in great cities and towns, and vagrants.

Upon a survey of the hearth books, made in Michaelmas, 1685, it was found that of the 1,300,000 houses in the whole kingdom, those of one chimney amounted to 554,631, but some of these having land about them, in all our calculations, we have computed the cottagers but at 500,000 families; but of these, a large number may get their own livelihood, and are no charge to the parish, for which reason Mr. King very judiciously computes his cottagers and paupers, decreasing the wealth of the nation but at 400,000 families, in which account he includes the poor-houses in cities, towns, and villages, besides which he reckons 30,000 vagrants, and all these together to make up 1,330,000 heads.

This is a very great proportion of the people to be a burden upon the other part, and is a weight upon the land interest, of which the landed gentlemen must certainly be very sensible.

If this vast body of men, instead of being expensive, could be rendered beneficial to the commonwealth, it were a work, no doubt, highly to be promoted by all who love their country.

It seems evident, to such as have considered these matters, and who have observed how they are ordered in nations under a good polity, that the number of such who through age or impotence stand in real need of relief, is but small and might be maintained for very little, and that the poor rates are swelled to the extravagant degree we now see them at by two sorts of people, one of which, by reason of our slack administration, is suffered to remain in sloth, and the other, through a defect in our constitution, continue in wretched poverty for want of employment, though willing enough to undertake it.

All this seems capable of a remedy, the laws may be armed against voluntary idleness, so as to prevent it, and a way may probably be found out to set those to work who are desirous to support themselves by their own labour; and if this could be brought about, it would not only put a stop to the course of that vice which is the consequence of an idle life, but it would greatly tend to enrich the commonwealth, for if the industry of not half the people maintain in some degree the other part, and, besides, in times of peace did add every year near two million and a half to the general stock of England, to what pitch of wealth and greatness might we not be brought, if one limb were not suffered to draw away the nourishment of the other, and if all the members of the body politic were rendered useful to it?

Nature, in her contrivances, has made every part of a living creature either for ornament or use; the same should be in a politic institution rightly governed.

It may be laid down for an undeniable truth, that where all work nobody will want, and to promote this would be a greater charity and more meritorious than to build hospitals, which very often are but so many monuments of ill-gotten riches attended with late repentance.

To make as many as possible of these 1,330,000 persons (whereof not above 330,000 are children too young to work) who now live chiefly upon others get themselves a large share of their maintenance would be the opening a new vein of treasure of some millions sterling per annum; it would be a present ease to every particular man of substance, and a lasting benefit to the whole body of the kingdom, for it would not only nourish but increase the numbers of the people, of which many thousands perish every year by those diseases contracted under a slothful poverty.

Our laws relating to the poor are very numerous, and this matter has employed the care of every age for a long time, though but with little success, partly through the ill execution, and partly through some defect in the very laws.

The corruptions of mankind are grown so great that, now-a-days, laws are not much observed which do not in a manner execute themselves; of this nature are those laws which relate to bringing in the Prince's revenue, which never fail to be put in execution, because the people must pay, and the Prince will be paid; but where only one part of the constitution, the people, are immediately concerned, as in laws relating to the poor, the highways, assizes, and other civil economy, and good order in the state, those are but slenderly regarded.

The public good being therefore, very often, not a motive strong enough to engage the magistrate to perform his duty, lawgivers have many times fortified their laws with penalties, wherein private persons may have a profit, thereby to stir up the people to put the laws in execution.

In countries depraved nothing proceeds well wherein particular men do not one way or other find their account; and rather than a public good should not go on at all, without doubt, it is better to give private men some interest to set it forward.

For which reason it may be worth the consideration of such as study the prosperity and welfare of England, whether this great engine of maintaining the poor, and finding them work and employment, may not be put in motion by giving some body of undertakers a reasonable gain to put the machine upon its wheels.

In order to which, we shall here insert a proposal delivered to the House of Commons last session of Parliament, for the better maintaining the impotent, and employing and setting to work the other poor of this kingdom.

In matters of this nature, it is always good to have some model or plan laid down, which thinking men may contemplate, alter, and correct, as they see occasion; and the writer of these papers does rather choose to offer this scheme, because he is satisfied it was composed by a gentleman of great abilities, and who has made both the poor rates, and their number, more his study than any other person in the nation. The proposal is as follows

A Scheme for Setting the Poor to Work.

First, that such persons as shall subscribe and pay the sum of 300,000 pounds as a stock for and towards the better maintaining the impotent poor, and for buying commodities and materials to employ and set at work the other poor, be incorporated and made one body politic, &c. By the name of the Governor and Company for Maintaining and Employing the Poor of this Kingdom.

By all former propositions, it was intended that the parishes should advance several years' rates to raise a stock, but by this proposal the experiment is to be made by private persons at their risk; and 300,000 pounds may be judged a very good stock, which, added to the poor rates for a certain number of years, will be a very good fund for buying commodities and materials for a million of money at any time. This subscription ought to be free for everybody, and if the sum were subscribed in the several counties of England and Wales, in proportion to their poor rates, or the monthly assessment, it would be most convenient; and provision may be made that no person shall transfer his interest but to one of the same county, which will keep the interest there during the term; and as to its being one Corporation, it is presumed this will be most beneficial to the public. For first, all disputes on removes, which are very chargeable and burthensome, will be at an end--this proposal intending, that wherever the poor are, they shall be maintained or employed. Secondly, it will prevent one county which shall be diligent, imposing on their neighbours who may be negligent, or getting away their manufactures from them. Thirdly, in case of fire, plague, or loss of manufacture, the stock of one county may not be sufficient to support the places where such calamities may happen; and it is necessary the whole body should support every particular member, so that hereby there will be a general care to administer to every place according to their necessities.

Secondly, that the said Corporation be established for the term of one-and-twenty years.

The Corporation ought to be established for one-and-twenty years, or otherwise it cannot have the benefit the law gives in case of infants, which is their service for their education; besides, it will be some years before a matter of this nature can be brought into practice.

Thirdly, that the said sum of 300,000 pounds be paid in, and laid out for the purposes aforesaid, to remain as a stock for and during the said term of one-and-twenty years.

The subscription ought to be taken at the passing of the Act, but the Corporation to be left at liberty to begin either the Michaelmas or the Lady Day after, as they shall think fit. And XXX per cent. to be paid at the subscribing to persons appointed for that purpose, and the remainder before they begin to act; but so as 300,000 pounds shall be always in stock during the term, notwithstanding any dividends or other disposition: and an account thereof to be exhibited twice in every year upon oath, before the Lord Chancellor for the time being.

Fourthly, that the said corporation do by themselves, or agents in every parish of England, from and after the XXX day of XXX during the said term of one-and-twenty years, provide for the real impotent poor good and sufficient maintenance and reception, as good or better than hath at any time within the space of XXX years before the said XXX day of XXX been provided or allowed to such impotent poor, and so shall continue to provide for such impotent poor, and what other growing impotent poor shall happen in the said parish during the said term.

By impotent poor is to be understood all infants and old and decrepid persons not able to work; also persons who by sickness or any accident are for the time unable to labour for themselves or families; and all persons (not being fit for labour) who were usually relieved by the money raised for the use of the poor; they shall have maintenance, as good or better, as within XXX years they used to have.

This does not directly determine what that shall be, nor is it possible, by reason a shilling in one county is as much as two in another; but it will be the interest of the Corporation that such poor be well provided for, by reason the contrary will occasion all the complaints or clamour that probably can be made against the Corporation.

Fifthly, that the Corporation do provide (as well for all such poor which on the said XXX day of XXX shall be on the poor books, as for what other growing poor shall happen in the said term who are or shall be able to labour or do any work) sufficient labour and work proper for such persons to be employed in. And that provision shall be made for such labouring persons according to their labour, so as such provision doth not exceed three-fourth parts as much as any other person would have paid for such labour. And in case they are not employed and set to work, then such persons shall, until materials or labour be provided for them, be maintained as impotent poor; but so as such persons who shall hereafter enter themselves on the poor's book, being able to labour, shall not quit the service of the corporation, without leave, for the space of six months.

The Corporation are to provide materials and labour for all that can work, and to make provision for them not exceeding three-fourth parts as much as any other person would give for such labour. For example, if another person would give one of these a shilling, the Corporation ought to give but ninepence. And the reason is plain, first, because the Corporation will be obliged to maintain them and their families in all exigences, which others are not obliged to do, and consequently they ought not to allow so much as others. Secondly, in case any persons able to labour, shall come to the Corporation, when their agents are not prepared with materials to employ them, by this proposal they are to allow them full provision as impotent poor, until they find them work, which is entirely in favour of the poor. Thirdly, it is neither reasonable nor possible for the Corporation to provide materials upon every occasion, for such persons as shall be entered with them, unless they can be secure of such persons to work up those materials; besides, without this provision, all the labouring people of England will play fast and loose between their employers and the Corporation, for as they are disobliged by one, they will run to the other, and so neither shall be sure of them.

Sixthly, that no impotent poor shall be removed out of the parish where they dwell, but upon notice in writing given to the churchwardens or overseers of the said parish, to what place of provision he or she is removed.

It is judged the best method to provide for the impotent poor in houses prepared for that purpose, where proper provision may be made for several, with all necessaries of care and maintenance. So that in some places one house will serve the impotent poor of several parishes, in which case the parish ought to know where to resort, to see if good provision be made for them.

Seventhly, that in case provision be not made for the poor of each parish, in manner as aforesaid (upon due notice given to the agents of the Corporation) the said parish may order their poor to be maintained, and deduct the sum by them expended out of the next payments to be made to the said corporation by the said parish.

In case any accident happens in a parish, either by sickness, fall, casualty of fire, or other ways; and that the agent of the Corporation is not present to provide for them, or having notice doth not immediately do it, the parish may do it, and deduct so much out of the next payment; but there must be provision made for the notice, and in what time the Corporation shall provide for them.

Eighthly, that the said Corporation shall have and receive for the said one-and-twenty years, that is to say, from every parish yearly, so much as such parish paid in any one year, to be computed by a medium of seven years; namely, from the 25th of March, 1690, to the 25th of March 1697, and to be paid half-yearly; and besides, shall receive the benefit of the revenues of all donations given to any parish, or which shall be given during the said term, and all forfeitures which the law gives to the use of the poor; and to all other sums which were usually collected by the parish, for the maintenance of the poor.

Whatever was raised for or applied to the use of the poor, ought to be paid over to the Corporation; and where there are any donations for maintaining the poor, it will answer the design of the donor, by reason there will be better provision for the maintenance of the poor than ever; and if that maintenance be so good, as to induce further charities, no doubt the Corporation ought to be entitled to them. But there are two objections to this article; first that to make a medium by a time of war is unreasonable. Secondly, to continue the whole tax for one-and-twenty years, does not seem to give any benefit to the kingdom in that time. To the first, it is true, we have a peace, but trade is lower now than at any time during the war, and the charge of the poor greater; and when trade will mend is very uncertain. To the second, it is very plain, that although the charge may be the same to a parish in the total, yet it will be less to particular persons, because those who before received alms, will now be enabled to be contributors; but besides, the turning so many hundred thousand pounds a year (which in a manner have hitherto been applied only to support idleness) into industry; and the employing so many other idle vagrants and sturdy beggars, with the product of their labour, will altogether be a present benefit to the lands of England, as well in the rents as in the value; and further the accidental charities in the streets and at doors, is, by a very modest computation, over and above the poor rates, at least 300,000 pounds per annum, which will be entirely saved by this proposal, and the persons set at work; which is a further consideration for its being well received, since the Corporation are not allowed anything for this service.

The greater the encouragement is, the better the work will be performed; and it will become the wisdom of the parliament in what they do, to make it effectual; for should such an undertaking as this prove ineffectual, instead of remedying, it will increase the mischief.

Ninthly, that all the laws made for the provision of the poor, and for punishing idle vagrant persons, be repealed, and one law made to continue such parts as are found useful, and to add such other restrictions, penalties, and provisions, as may effectually attain the end of this great work.

The laws hereunto relating are numerous, but the judgment and opinions given upon them are so various and contradictory, and differ so in sundry places, as to be inconsistent with any one general scheme of management.

Tenthly, that proper persons be appointed in every county to determine all matters and differences which may arise between the corporation and the respective parishes.

To prevent any ill usage, neglect or cruelty, it will be necessary to make provision that the poor may tender their complaints to officers of the parish; and that those officers having examined the same, and not finding redress, may apply to persons to be appointed in each county and each city for that purpose, who may be called supervisors of the poor, and may have allowance made them for their trouble; and their business may be to examine the truth of such complaints; and in case either the parish or corporation judge themselves aggrieved by the determination of the said supervisors, provision may be made that an appeal lie to the quarter sessions.

Eleventhly, that the corporation be obliged to provide for all public beggars, and to put the laws into execution against public beggars and idle vagrant persons.

Such of the public beggars as can work must be employed, the rest to be maintained as impotent poor, but the laws to be severely put in execution against those who shall ask any public alms.

This proposal, which in most parts of it seems to be very maturely weighed, may be a foundation for those to build upon who have a public spirit large enough to embrace such a noble undertaking.

But the common obstruction to anything of this nature is a malignant temper in some who will not let a public work go on if private persons are to be gainers by it. When they are to get themselves, they abandon all sense of virtue; but are clothed in her whitest robe when they smell profit coming to another, masking themselves with a false zeal to the commonwealth, where their own turn is not to be served. It were better, indeed, that men would serve their country for the praise and honour that follow good actions, but this is not to be expected in a nation at least leaning towards corruption, and in such an age it is as much as we can hope for if the prospect of some honest gain invites people to do the public faithful service. For which reason, in any undertaking where it can be made apparent that a great benefit will accrue to the commonwealth in general, we ought not to have an evil eye upon what fair advantages particular men may thereby expect to reap, still taking care to keep their appetite of getting within moderate bounds, laying all just and reasonable restraints upon it, and making due provision that they may not wrong or oppress their fellow subjects.

It is not to be denied, but that if fewer hands were suffered to remain idle, and if the poor had full employment, it would greatly tend to the common welfare, and contribute much towards adding every year to the general stock of England.

Among the methods that we have here proposed of employing the poor, and making the whole body of the people useful to the public, we think it our duty to mind those who consider the common welfare of looking with a compassionate eye into the prisons of this kingdom, where many thousands consume their time in vice and idleness, wasting the remainder of their fortunes, or lavishing the substance of their creditors, eating bread and doing no work, which is contrary to good order, and pernicious to the commonwealth.

We cannot therefore but recommend the thoughts of some good bill that may effectually put an end to this mischief so scandalous in a trading country, which should let no hands remain useless.

It is not at all difficult to contrive such a bill as may relieve and release the debtor, and yet preserve to his creditors all their fair, just, and honest rights and interest.

And so we have in this matter endeavoured to show that to preserve and increase the people, and to make their numbers useful, are methods conducing to make us gainers in the balance of trade.

###

Printed in the USA
CPSIA information can be obtained
at www.ICGtesting.com
LVHW082105021223
765382LV00005B/695